Embracing the Power of Cloud Hosting for Banking Solutions

A Handful Guide for Professionals

Balagopal Thotakura
Rashmi Gupta

Embracing the Power of Cloud Hosting for Banking Solutions
A Handful Guide for Professionals

Editor: Sowmya
Production Manager: Meghna
Cover design by Freepik and Vecteezy
Formatting & Indexing: Gaurav Mutreja

First Edition: Sep-2024

Reference: 2401017

Published by Arcchie Publications

ISBN-13 (paperback): 978-81-974190-0-3
ISBN-13 (eBook): 978-81-974190-9-6

www.arcchieonline.com

FOREWORD

I am honored to write this foreword as this topic is very close to my heart. Having spent over 25 years in the financial industry embracing its multi-pronged transformations from internet trading to crypto exchanges, from back-office automation to Gen AI chatbots and from legacy platforms to hybrid cloud architectures, I can arguably state that cloud transformation journey has been one of the most disruptive technology trends for the banking industry. The cloud transformation journey has made the industry a level playing field allowing focus on differentiated product and service experiences that ultimately will benefit the end customer.

I am also grateful that Rashmi Gupta and T Bala Gopal decided to harness their deep technical knowledge and banking domain expertise in this eloquent and concise book, as it will help both novices and industry experts to hone their cloud transformation skills.

This comprehensive book covers both the financial domain knowledge and the technological details about transforming Banking IT solutions to cloud. It provides a thorough introduction to the financial industry, evolution of banking industry with some real-life examples and the associated regulatory requirements in the financial sector. The book also explains the implementation of cloud IT solutions for banks and in-depth coverage of cloud migration strategies. Additionally, the book explores the transformative power of new technologies in the financial sector and discusses sustainability initiatives aimed at reducing the environmental footprint of cloud IT operations. It also details the cybersecurity, risk and compliance aspects of the industry as cloud journeys are considered. Featuring expert insights, real-world case studies, and practical guidance, this book equips professionals with the knowledge and tools needed to succeed in the rapidly evolving world of financial technology.

I am sure you will find this book extremely practical as you evaluate the various facets of your cloud transformation journey and will provide a useful playbook for execution.

Enjoy!

Rashmi Das,
Global Financial Services Leader
Business Transformation services

ACKNOWLEDGMENT

We would like to extend our sincere appreciation to the team at Arcchie Publications for their unwavering support and guidance throughout the publication process of this book. Their expertise in editorial services, marketing, and distribution significantly contributed to the overall quality and reach of the final product. The Publisher's vision and belief in the book's worthiness have been instrumental in bringing this project to life.

Our Mentor Gaurav Arora's guidance and mentorship throughout the writing process have been invaluable. His wealth of knowledge and experience in the field have provided direction, inspiration, and valuable insights.

We would also like to thank our leaders, colleagues, friends and family members for their support and encouragement. Their faith in our abilities and the book's relevance has inspired us to strive for excellence and contribute meaningfully to this book.

- Balagopal Thotakura, Rashmi Gupta

ABOUT THE AUTHORS

- **Balagopal Thotakura** is a highly accomplished and experienced IT professional with over two and half decades of hands-on expertise in the field. Throughout his illustrious career, he has demonstrated exceptional technical leadership qualities and comes with a proven track record in architecting and implementing complex solutions for prestigious clients across multiple industry verticals, including finance, insurance, telecom, electronics, and banking. He comes with experience of successfully delivering complex solutions for prominent banking clients across North America and Australia. His core competencies lie in delivering high-quality solutions based on open standards and integrating disparate technologies to create cohesive and efficient ecosystems. Balagopal holds several esteemed certifications, including OpenGroup Master Certified Architect and OpenGroup Master Certified Technical Specialist, as well as Google Cloud Certified - Professional Cloud Architect and AWS Certified Solutions Architect – Associate. These accolades reflect his commitment to staying abreast of emerging trends and maintaining mastery over industry-leading tools and frameworks. Currently employed as a Senior Solution Architect as a prominent IT MNC, Balagopal specializes in implementing sophisticated solutions for clients, leveraging his extensive domain knowledge and cross-functional skillset. His vast experience enables him to lead teams effectively, manage projects efficiently, and deliver results that meet and exceed client expectations. Overall, Balagopal Thotakura represents a rare blend of technical prowess, business acumen, and interpersonal skills, with a proven proficiency in delivering solutions across multiple industry verticals, coupled with his strong leadership capabilities, ensures the timely delivery of high-quality output that meets and exceeds client satisfaction criteria.

- **Rashmi Gupta** is an accomplished and experienced IT professional with over 27 years of experience, predominantly focused on the finance and retail sectors. Holding a bachelor's degree in computer science and the Management course from IIM Kolkata, Rashmi has established herself as a trusted and result-oriented professional. Throughout her career, she has held influential positions in renowned organizations and has been part of regular interactions and strategic discussions with Executive Leadership. At present, she works as an Associate Partner with a multinational company, spearheading and managing global sales and deliveries for the US-based financial services client.

Rashmi has partnered on pioneering solutions in the hybrid cloud and AI spaces, showcasing her expertise in harnessing cutting-edge technologies to address complex business challenges. She excels in bringing value added and innovative solutions for the stakeholders, by collaborating closely with business and engineering teams and driving digital transformation and product engineering initiatives. She is a keen learner and holds multiple management and cloud certifications. She is also a certified Generative AI Sales and Hybrid Cloud Knowledge Leader. These recognitions highlight her steadfast commitment to professional development and her capacity to excel in dynamic business environments.

ABOUT THE TECHNICAL REVIEWERS

- **Shalu Mehta** is an experienced IT leader with over 20 years of experience, specializing in managing large-scale, complex programs across various domains. Her expertise extends to leading and optimizing offshore and onshore delivery operations, strategic account and program management, cloud transformations, quality assurance, and developing strategic roadmaps for new programs. Shalu's strong focus on digitization, process optimization, automation, and GenAI is complemented by her unwavering commitment to implementing Agile methodologies and DevOps principles, thereby improving efficiency and effectiveness.

- **Aishwarya Gupta** is a consulting leader at Microsoft with over 23 years of experience in Apps, Data, and Artificial Intelligence. She specializes in Strategy Consulting, Enterprise Transformation, and Product and Program Management and consistently drives business growth. Currently leading a consulting team at Microsoft, Aishwarya is known for her customer-focused approach and has been instrumental in securing new clients through strategic partnerships. A passionate advocate for diversity, she mentors' women in tech, earning recognition as the Best Woman Leader in Tech by Analytics India Magazine. Her contributions to the tech industry have also been acknowledged with the "SHE Achiever's Award" from Shiksha Ek Pahal NGO and commendations from industry leaders like Azim Premji for her AI consulting expertise. Aishwarya has collaborated with premier educational institutions, including IIT Madras, where she reviewed their Data Science and Machine Learning curriculum, aiming to bridge the skills gap between academia and industry. She is also the author of "AI for Everyone," a NASSCOM-published booklet, and has been a panelist at major events hosted by Microsoft, Google, and IBM. Her work in digital business strategy, particularly in Apps and AI Solutions, has defined successful go-to-market strategies and pricing models for digital assets. Aishwarya's expertise in Strategy and marketing, coupled with her commitment to a customer-first philosophy, has made her a key player in the tech industry. She holds executive education credentials in Leading Customer Growth from Wharton Business School and Brand Management from London Business School.

PREFACE

As the banking industry continues to evolve, it needs to navigate the complexities of digital transformation. The need for secure, scalable, and agile infrastructure to support the banking IT solutions has never been more pressing. The banking industry stands at the precipice of a technological revolution, driven by the relentless march towards digital transformation and the insatiable demand for seamless, personalized experiences. Amidst these shifts, cloud hosting has emerged as a transformative force and has emerged as a game-changer in this regard, offering financial institutions the ability to deploy mission-critical applications and data with unprecedented scalability, flexibility and reliability. In this book, we explore the rapidly evolving landscape of cloud hosting for banking solutions. The journey starts with explaining how the Financial Sector and Banking Industries have evolved over time. We then explore the technical considerations of cloud migration and deployment, the strategic implications of cloud adoption for financial institutions and shedding light on the critical factors influencing successful cloud migrations and adoptions. Further, we delve into the latest trends, best practices, and expert insights that are shaping the future of cloud-based banking. With the rise of cloud-native applications, the increasing adoption of DevOps and agile development methodologies, and the growing importance of data analytics and artificial intelligence in banking, the need for cloud-based solutions has never been more urgent. This book provides a comprehensive guide to the technical, operational, and strategic aspects of cloud hosting for banking solutions, including:

- The foundational concepts of the banking industry, the regulations and the challenges being faced.
- The benefits and challenges of cloud adoption in the banking industry
- The key considerations for cloud migration and deployment
- The role of cloud in enabling digital transformation and innovation
- The importance of security, compliance, and risk management in cloud-based banking
- Real-world case studies and expert insights from Functional and Technical leaders.

This book covers the functional, technical and regulatory concepts from basics all the way to advanced discussions. Whether you're a banking executive looking to stay ahead of the curve, a technology professional seeking to understand the latest trends and best practices, or simply interested in the future of cloud-based banking, this book is your authoritative guide to the rapidly evolving world of cloud hosting for banking solutions.

Welcome to the journey.

Let's embark on this journey of learning together.

What's Inside This Book

Chapter 1: Introduction sets the context for the book and provides an overview of the subsequent chapters.

Chapter 2: Financial Services Landscape provides a quick rundown of the financial sector, including its main parts, the services it offers, and some famous companies involved. It also discusses Fintech—a term that means using technology to improve financial services—and explains how it influences the financial industry.

Chapter 3: Evolution of Banking Industry explores the historical evolution of the banking industry, tracing its roots back to ancient civilizations and charting its progression through the Industrial Revolution and beyond. It also highlights the crucial role of Information Technology (IT) in transforming contemporary banking and discusses the revolutionary impact of mobile banking.

Chapter 4: Introduction to Cloud Computing emphasizes the fundamental concepts of cloud computing, detailing its defining traits, comparative advantages over on-premises server setups, and diverse service and deployment options. It also sheds light on cloud native technologies and their essential attributes.

Chapter 5: Challenges of moving Banking workloads to Cloud focuses on the distinctive features and obstacles associated with cloud migration in the banking sector. It addresses vital security concerns, compliance requirements, and potential risks inherent in the process. Moreover, it examines common causes of failed cloud migrations and offers recommendations to mitigate them.

Chapter 6: Designing Banking Cloud Solutions delves into designing a banking cloud solution, discussing the various cloud alternatives available and advocating for hybrid cloud architectures tailored to the banking industry. It also outlines best practices and common mistakes to avoid during the cloud implementation process.

Chapter 7: Designing Cloud Solutions – Deep Dive explores in depth cloud solutions, drawing on practical use cases from the banking sector to illustrate key principles and techniques. By examining real-world successes and failures, readers can benefit from actionable advice and valuable lessons learned.

Chapter 8: Security, Risk and Compliance underscores the paramount of security, risk mitigation, and regulatory alignment in banking cloud solutions. It begins by outlining essential security considerations and proceeds to discuss the design of resilient banking systems that prioritize cybersecurity. Following this, it explores prevalent risks, proposing methods for assessment and mitigation. Lastly, it reviews compliance requirements and highlights necessary actions for adhering to them.

Chapter 9: Peek into the future delves into recent advancements and foresighted approaches in the IT landscape for the banking industry. It evaluates the merits and drawbacks of adopting cutting-edge technologies and discusses how their integration could facilitate the creation of next-generation solutions for the sector.

Chapter 10: Sustainable Technology Solutions emphasizes the significance of balancing technological progress with environmental responsibility in the banking industry. It introduces the concept of green IT and explores eco-friendly practices in implementing and disposing of equipment, thereby contributing to a sustainable future.

For Whom This Book Is Intended

This book is designed for:

- Novice enthusiasts seeking to understand the financial services landscape and associated security and compliance requirements.
- Business Analysts looking for deep financial sector concepts.
- Technologists working on design of Banking solutions and cloud migrations.
- Tech innovators and architects are looking to mitigate the challenges of cloud deployments and implement the best practices.
- Business Leaders and Entrepreneurs keen on exploring futuristic solutions.

Download the source code and colored images:

To download the source code bundle

and the colored images, please follow the link

OR

scan the QR Code

https://l1nq.com/2t8Ld

Errata

At **ARCCHIE Publications**, we are committed to delivering the highest-quality content in all our publications. We follow best practices to ensure the accuracy of our content to provide our readers with an indulgent reading experience. We believe and understand that our readers are our best judges, and we always use their input and feedback from time to time to improve human errors, if any, that may occur during the publishing processes involved. We invite you to participate in our errata submission process to ensure our books remain accurate and up to date. Please help us reach out to readers who might have difficulties due to unforeseen errors. Please write to us at *errata@arcchieonline.com*.

When submitting errata, please include the following information:

- Book Title

- Reference#

- Author(s)

- Page Number

- Description of the Error

- Suggested Correction (if applicable)

The **ARCCHIE Publications** Family highly appreciates your support, suggestions, and feedback.

Sharing Your Perspective and Providing Feedback

Your perspective is invaluable to us, as it helps us enhance our content and gather your feedback. We warmly welcome all forms of feedback. Please feel free to send us an email at `feedback@arcchieonline.com`, mentioning the book title in the subject line of your message.

Book Review Invitation

We kindly invite you to share your thoughts. After you've read and engaged with this book, consider leaving a review on the platform where you acquired it. Your impartial feedback can greatly assist potential readers in making informed decisions. Your reviews provide valuable insights for us at `Arcchie`, helping us better understand your perspectives on our products, and they offer authors the chance to appreciate your feedback on their work.

PIRACY

Should you encounter unauthorized reproductions of our publications in any digital format on the internet, we kindly request your assistance in pinpointing their locations or website sources. Please reach out to us at `copyright@arcchieonline.com` and include a link to the infringing material.

If you possess expertise in a particular subject and wish to participate in the creation or contribution to a book, please visit *authors.arcchieonline.com*. We welcome you and assist you to start your authorship journey with `ARCCHIE PUBLICATIONS`.

JOIN US ON THE
ARCCHIE PUBLICATIONS
DISCORD SERVER

Connect with fellow readers, authors, and enthusiasts to discuss all things related to our publications and the exciting world of AI, programming, and learning. Share your insights, ask questions, and engage in vibrant discussions to expand your knowledge and inspire creativity. Take advantage of this opportunity to be part of a dynamic community dedicated to exploring the frontiers of technology and innovation. Join our Discord Server today and be part of the ARCCHIE Publications community!

https://discord.gg/z26SenmpEt

TABLE OF CONTENTS

Chapter 1
Introduction

In this chapter, we will get a glance at the topics that will be covered in this book. We will familiarize ourselves with the financial sector and the importance of security and compliance, which are crucial for ensuring the safety of financial transactions. We will discuss the upcoming IT trends impacting banking applications, such as AI and blockchain, and take a sneak peek into what cloud computing means and its characteristics, which are revolutionizing the way IT services are delivered. Each of these topics will be covered in detail in the subsequent chapters.

In this chapter we have a very high-level overview about

- Financial Industry
- Cloud Computing
- Security and Compliance
- IT Trends in Banking

Financial Industry

Financial Industry has been in existence in some form or other from the beginning of mankind. It has evolved significantly over centuries from simple activities like exchanging goods (barter system) to very complex transactions that span different geographies and multiple parties. This journey has been quite interesting with many different practices evolving as industry spread across the different parts of the world.

Financial activity is inherently risky. To maintain trust and protect against malign activities, standardization and enforcing regulations become critical with increasing adaptation and scope. There are many essential Financial Services Regulations like GDPR, PCI DSS, SOX etc. which are mandatory for the financial institutes to follow. Some of these regulations are specific to a region. We will understand these in more detail in Chapter 2 of this book.

Looking at the current banking system, we may not realize how much it has evolved since its inception. From the Ancient banks in 2000 BC to the new era of modern banking, Financial Industry has come a long way and has seen its fair share of ups and downs. All of which has contributed significantly towards current landscape and advancements.

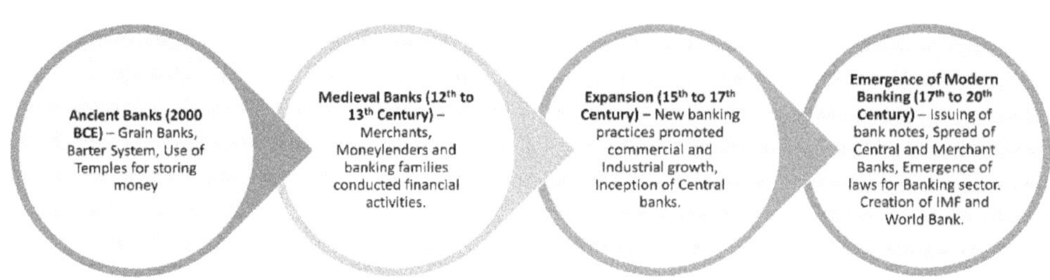

Figure 1.1: History of Banking

With the massive growth and evolving scenarios, technological advancements came to the rescue. For decades, the banking sector has maintained its position at the forefront of modern technological advancement. The use of computers in banking in the 1960s sparked the first digital banking revolution. Online banking started making headway in the late 1990's and 2000, as the digital portals could be accessed over the phone line. The enhanced use of smartphones in the late 2000s and early 2010s led to the emergence of mobile banking. With growing internet penetration and digitalization, banking sectors have made innovative shifts to address the consumer's needs. We will discuss the evolution of the Banking Industry in detail in Chapter 3 of this week.

Cloud Computing

By delivering banking services over the Internet, banks have managed to advance their offerings and attract a large consumer base. In today's dynamic banking landscape, digital transformation is taking center stage, driven by the rising demand for seamless and personalized customer experiences.

The supporting systems have become more resource intensive with growing computer power and memory requirements. This has led to the evolution of cloud computing for leveraging shared resources across multiple clients, to result in cost reduction and enforce standardization by using best practices. It is important to understand that this is not a one-shot solution to solve all the Bank's IT Problems.

Cloud computing is a paradigm shift from traditional computing solutions. So, it is critical that they are designed well to meet the basic purpose – cost reduction and building efficient systems. The journey begins with analysis to evaluate and plan for what to migrate (what not to migrate), why to migrate and how to migrate to cloud. These technological advancements come with their challenges. The Cloud Computing platform is quite mature now and there are a variety of tools available to assist at each stage.

The key characteristics of Cloud Computing are achieving the economies of scale by pooling the resources, multi-tenancy by sharing the resources, virtualization, On-demand self-service etc. which acts as powerful tools to build a robust, secure, scalable and cost-efficient solution on cloud.

Depending on where the applications are deployed, how they are managed and who do they share information with the following cloud deployments models can be used – Private Cloud, Public Cloud, Hybrid Cloud, Multi Cloud etc. We will cover in detail more about the Cloud Computing concepts and cloud native technologies Chapter 4 of this book.

Implementing the IT cloud solutions for financial industry comes with its own set of challenges, primarily due to technological shift, regulations, cyber security, evolving customer expectations and cultural shift. If not handled holistically, sometimes the cloud adaptation may fail because of the improper design, ineffective governance or even lack of vision. To help organizations overcome their cloud adaptation challenges, the major Cloud Providers provide guiding architectural principles and reusable frameworks to guide the tenants on their cloud adoption.

To develop a new application from scratch on cloud generally have a systematic approach and is easier to plan. On the contrary, migrating the existing application to cloud involves dealing with the technological and functional limitations of the existing applications. As a result, a detailed assessment of the existing application needs to be performed, and a suitable migration framework is identified for each of the applications. The six popular strategies available are Retain, Re-host, Retire, Re-platform, Re-factoring and Re-Purchase.

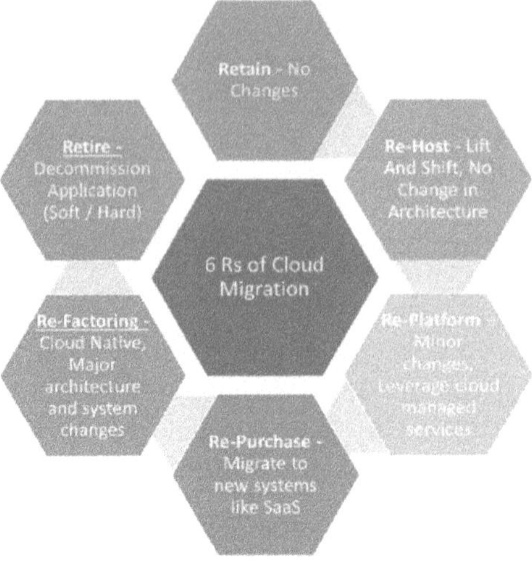

Figure 1.2: 6Rs of Cloud Migration

There are different types of cloud offerings, and multiple vendors in the market offering various competitive solutions. We must consider all the options to choose the right fit, which could even involve engaging multiple cloud offerings. The possible solutions would be different for each use case and scenario. For many applications, the primary driving force for cloud implementation may be to reduce the infrastructure cost, but that should not be the only factor to consider. Implementing a cloud solution does not mean hosting an existing legacy application onto new shared infrastructure. Though this may be a good first step to help reduce infrastructure costs, cloud offers various services for achieving flexibility and efficiency, in a cost-effective way. The full potential of the cloud lies in using appropriate services. Cloud adaptation provides many benefits that should be leveraged to build a more secure, available, scalable, and efficient system.

Cloud Providers offer a wide range of services that usually can cater to most of the use cases. Some of the key ones are as follows:

- Geographical Hosting Options
- Compute Services
- Storage Services
- Data Processing
- Security
- DevOps Services
- System Integration
- Networking
- Load Balancing

Depending on the complexity of migration and the specific scenario we are dealing with, the short term and long-term strategy for the application and data migration is decided. We will discuss some of the use cases and the best practices in detail in Chapter 7 of this book.

Security, Risk and Compliance

As the ease of banking increases due to widespread automation, like ATMs and Mobile Banking, so are the inherent risks. There have always been fraudsters with malicious intentions to exploit the vulnerabilities in the system, like cyber criminals using sophisticated techniques like phishing to lure unsuspecting customers to gain control of their valuable assets. Hence cybersecurity becomes critical to safeguards the banks and its customers from incurring financial losses.

It is important to understand the risks associated with banking solutions and implement ways to effectively assess and mitigate them. There are compliance and regulatory requirements enforced by government authorities to help banking organizations to overcome these issues.

There are two main types of risks that impact the financial sector

- Financial Risks associated with banking sector.
- Technology related risks impacting banking applications.

In this book we are focusing on the IT solutions for Banking. Hence, we will concentrate on Technology related risks and how to mitigate them. Some of the key technology related risks are:

- Loss of data
- Software Defect/ Application Malfunction
- Regulatory Risks
- Cyber Threats
- In-effective IT Strategy

Chapter 8 of this book will cover in detail the types of risk, Risk analysis and mitigation and the best practices which can be adapted.

IT Trends in Banking

Services provided to customers evolve and as time progresses, 'nice-to-have' features soon become 'must-have' features. For example, ATM was first provisioned into service around 1960's, before that customers could not have imagined this service where they can do cash transactions 24 X 7

, without hinderance of bank holidays. Or, at the end of 20th century, who would have imagined about the features provided by mobile banking with the ability to avail most of the banking services by click of a button would be available at your fingertips. Now we have banks offering personalized services, by 'understanding' what the customer likes – even before the customer asks for it. Such Hyper Personalization is possible with the current and emerging technological advancements in Machine Learning and Artificial Intelligence.

Keeping up with trends in the rapidly expanding realm of technology is critical, and the financial sector has always been at the forefront of technological advancements. There are several innovative advancements predicted to revolutionize the technology sector even further. Some of the emerging trends we are witnessing are:

- Deeper Integration of AI/ML in Financial Applications
- Implementation of Gen AI in real life use cases
- Hyper Personalization
- Focus on Enhanced Cyber- Security
- Quantum Computing Advancements
- Blockchain and Crypto currencies
- Fintech and Insurtech being adapted in mainstream.

These trends may have a significant impact on banking applications over the coming years. All these technological advancements come with a cost to the environment, with the amount of electricity they consume, the heat the computing generates, the electronic waste that is created in the process, etc. Responsibility lies with the cloud service providers, banking organizations and the end consumers in minimizing the impact to the environment and focusing on sustainable computing.

Conclusion

In this chapter, we had a high-level overview about the financial sector, cloud computing characteristics and the upcoming trends in IT impacting banking applications. Each of these will be discussed in detail in the subsequent chapters. The future of IT applications in banking is exciting and full of opportunities, but it's also rapidly changing. Financial institutions would be required to take a strategic and balanced approach to embrace new technologies, comply with changing regulations, and adapt to changing consumer preferences. In the next Chapter, we will focus more on the type of financial organizations, industry regulations and the Fintech revolution.

Chapter 2
Financial Services Landscape

The financial services sector is a cornerstone of modern economies, acting as the backbone that supports both individual and corporate financial activities. This intricate landscape encompasses a vast array of services and institutions that facilitate the flow of capital, manage risks, and enable wealth creation and preservation. As we delve into this chapter, we will explore the multifaceted world of financial services, highlighting its key components, functions, and the dynamic interplay between various entities within the sector.

Key Components of Financial Services

At its core, the financial services landscape is built upon a diverse set of components, each playing a crucial role in the overall functionality of the economy. These components are not isolated, but rather interconnected, forming a complex ecosystem that drives economic activity.

- **Banking**: The traditional cornerstone of financial services, banking institutions provide a wide range of services, including deposit-taking, lending, and payment processing. Commercial banks, investment banks, and retail banks form the pillars of this segment.
- **Insurance**: Insurance companies offer protection against various risks, from health and life to property and liability. This segment helps individuals and businesses mitigate potential financial losses.
- **Investment** Services include asset management firms, mutual funds, hedge funds, and private equity firms. These entities manage investments for individuals and institutions, aiming to generate returns and grow wealth.

- **Securities and Trading**: Stock exchanges, brokerage firms, and trading platforms facilitate the buying and selling of financial securities, including stocks, bonds, and derivatives. This segment ensures liquidity and price discovery in financial markets.
- **Financial Technology (FinTech)**: The advent of technology has revolutionized the financial services sector. FinTech companies, at the forefront of this innovation, leverage technology to offer innovative solutions in areas such as payments, lending, and wealth management, enhancing efficiency and accessibility and opening new possibilities in the financial world, promising an exciting future for the industry.

In this chapter we will discuss:

- An overview to Financial Services Industry
- Types of Financial Organizations
- Financial Services Industry Regulations
- Fintech Revolution

An overview to Financial Service Industry

Financial Services is used to describe the offerings within the finance industry, such as banking, mortgages, credit cards, payment services, tax preparation and planning, insurance, and investing. The financial services industry is one of the most important sectors of the economy. It caters to businesses, corporations, banks, and other financial institutions that provide financial services and sustain the economy.

We have seen rapid growth in the Financial Industry in the last few decades. This can primarily be attributed to Economic Globalization and Technology advancements. Substantial changes in the late 19th century created an environment favorable to the increase in and development of international financial centers.

The world economy became increasingly financially integrated in the 1980s and 1990s due to capital account liberalization and financial deregulation. In addition to Geopolitical factors, the impact of Information Technology, deregulation, and liberalization has changed and reshaped the economic landscape forever.

After the Second World War, there was an increased focus on technology. The Financial Institutes foresaw enormous benefits from leveraging the technology invented for the world war. The first credit card, called "Charge-It," was invented by John Biggins in 1946. Financial Institutes, especially Banks, started investing heavily in computers in the 1950s. Many large banks brought mainframe computers to process a large set of transactions. In the late 1950s, magnetic ink character recognition, or MICR, was introduced to expedite cheque clearing.

A significant technological revolution happened in 1967 when Barclays Bank installed an ATM in London. This revolutionary technology-enabled access to cash and banks at every block. This revelation of convenience was a game changer. Customers started demanding even more convenience. 1980 saw the emergence of telephone banking. The change of pace has continued since then.

In the current landscape, banking IT is rapidly evolving and influenced by various technological advancements, regulatory requirements, and shifting customer expectations. Some key developments that have and are shaping the industry are :

1. **Digital Transformation**: Banks have undergone a significant digital transformation, focusing on modernizing their technology infrastructure, streamlining processes, and enhancing customer experience. This includes the adoption of cloud computing, artificial intelligence, and machine learning.
2. **Cloud Migration**: Cloud computing has become increasingly popular in the banking industry, enabling greater flexibility, scalability, and cost savings. Many banks are migrating their applications and data to the cloud, leveraging public, private, or hybrid cloud models.
3. **Open Banking and APIs**: Open banking initiatives, such as the EU's PSD2 and the UK's Open Banking Standard, are promoting the use of application programming interfaces (APIs) to facilitate secure data sharing and collaboration between banks and fintech companies.
4. **Artificial Intelligence and Machine Learning**: AI and ML are being used in banking to enhance customer service, improve risk management, and streamline processes. Chatbots, natural language processing, and predictive analytics are some of the key areas of application.
5. **Mobile Banking and Digital Channels**: Mobile banking apps and digital channels are becoming increasingly popular, allowing customers to manage their accounts, make transactions, and access financial services remotely.
6. **Partnerships and Collaborations**: The banking industry is witnessing increased partnerships and collaborations between banks, fintech companies, and technology providers to leverage each other's strengths and stay competitive.
7. **Risk Management**: Banks are adopting advanced risk management techniques, including predictive analytics, machine learning, and behavioral modeling, to identify and mitigate potential risks.

Another critical factor transforming the financial services industry is bank consolidations through mergers and acquisitions. This is primarily motivated by:

- **The need for a large capital base**: This increases the institution's credibility, indirectly resulting in enhanced customer confidence.
- **Increase in Client Base**: With the increased capital, banks can offer greater financial commitments and, hence, attract more customers.
- **Optimized Cost of Operations**: The growing cost of technology, information, and communication is overwhelming, especially for small and mid-sized institutes.
- **Increased Profitability**: Focus on increased return on capital and assets.
- **Financial Stability of the economy**: Smaller banks with weak financial health, when absorbed by larger, more stable banks, can strengthen the economic stability of the banking system, reducing the risk of economic crises.

Private equity (PE) and venture capital (VC) play a significant role in driving mergers and acquisitions (M&A) in the financial services sector. Some of the ways in which they contribute are:

1. **Strategic acquisitions**: PE and VC firms often acquire companies to strengthen their portfolio companies or to create a platform for further growth.
2. **Financial support**: PE and VC firms can provide financial support to companies in the financial services sector, enabling them to grow through acquisitions. This support can take the form of equity or debt financing, allowing companies to expand their operations and make strategic acquisitions.
3. **Industry consolidation**: PE and VC firms identify opportunities for consolidation in the financial services sector by merging smaller companies to create a more efficient and competitive entity.
4. **Operational expertise**: PE and VC firms often bring operational expertise to the companies they invest in, which can help drive growth and efficiency.
5. **Risk capital**: PE and VC firms can provide risk capital to companies in the financial. They also have exit strategies in place, such as an initial public offering (IPO) or a sale to a strategic buyer.

Further, Geopolitical factors such as trade wars and economic sanctions significantly impacts the financial services industry. They can lead to increased market volatility, making it more challenging for financial institutions to make accurate predictions and manage risk. This can result in losses for investors and increased uncertainty for financial markets.

Trade wars can disrupt global supply chains impacting access to good and services, thus leading to increased cost and reduced profits. Economic sanctions can lead to changes in regulatory environments, making it more challenging for financial institutions to comply with new rules and regulations.

The financial sector is extensive and comprehensive, encompassing many types of businesses, from investments to taxes, accounting, insurance, banking, and more. In the next section, lets understand about the different types of financial organizations and the services they offer.

Types of Financial Organizations

There are many different types of financial organizations, and each has its unique set of services and products that it offers to the consumers.

We will discuss these types in the following list:

Insurance Companies

Insurance companies are the financial institutions that sell Insurance to the consumers to protect them against future losses. The insurance contracts manage the risks against the unforeseen incidents (like theft, accidents, loss of life or assets etc.) that may occur at a later point of time.

There are two main parties in "Insurance" – "The Insurer" and " The Insured". The Insurer guarantees payment for an uncertain future event, and "The insured or the policyholder" pays a smaller premium to the insurer in exchange for protection to cover potential risk in the future. The premium paid by the policyholder is used to run the insurance companies. Insurance companies pool the premiums of all their policyholders together, which is then used to pay claims.

Insurance companies serve both individuals and businesses, and they offer a wide range of products and services. Among the largest categories of insurance companies are accident and health insurers, property and casualty insurers, and financial guarantors. The most common personal insurance policies are auto, health, homeowners, and life.

The insurance industry is governed to guarantee consumer safety, monetary stability, ethical business practices, and adherence to solvency criteria.

Retail and Commercial Banks

Commercial banking is another name for corporate banking, which offers banking services to businesses, governments, and other institutions. These types of banks often provide a more comprehensive range of products than retail banks since retail banking is a typical subdivision of commercial banking. Commercial banking is fundamental to global economies.

The types of products and services commercial banks provide to businesses and institutions include:

- Checking and savings accounts
- Lines of credit
- Business loans
- Foreign exchange services
- Wealth management services

Retail or consumer banking involves financial products and services designed for families, individuals, and certain small businesses. The types of products and services available at most retail banks for individual consumers include:

- Checking and savings accounts
- Debit cards
- Credit cards
- Mortgages
- Personal loans

`Info`: The industry's best-known banks are in this category: Citi, Bank of America, Chase, and Wells Fargo offer both retail and commercial banking services.

Investment Banks

Investment banking is the division of a bank that works primarily with corporate and institutional customers by helping them with activities like investing, raising capital and arranging mergers and acquisitions. Investment banks carry out complex financial services and transactions on behalf of their clients by acting as underwriters and intermediaries.

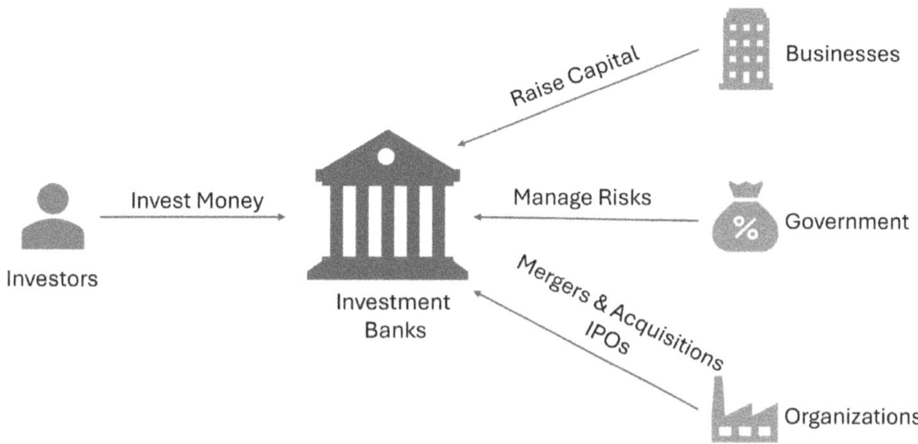

Figure 2.1: Investment Banking

The central banks in investment banking are Barclays Capital, Credit Suisse, Deutsche Bank, Goldman Sachs, J.P. Morgan, Morgan Stanley, and UBS.

Credit Unions

A credit union is a type of financial institution owned and operated by its members. It offers many of the same services as banks, but it is typically much smaller and more localized. Credit unions are not-for-profit organizations, which means that they do not have shareholders who expect to earn a return on their investment. Instead, credit unions use their profits to benefit their members through better rates and lower fees.

Credit unions follow a basic business model. Members pool their money (technically, they buy shares in the cooperative) to provide loans, demand deposit accounts, and other financial products and services to each other.

Credit unions have two distinct advantages over banks, both resulting from their status as nonprofit organizations:

- Credit unions are exempt from paying corporate income tax on earnings.
- Credit unions need to generate only enough earnings to fund daily operations. As a result, they can work with narrower operating margins than banks, where shareholders expect to increase earnings every quarter.

Usually, credit unions offer higher rates on interest-bearing accounts, lower rates on loans, lower fees, and a more personal touch regarding customer service.

Disadvantages of Credit Unions vs. Banks

- Fewer Locations
- Lower Tech
- Limited Products and Services
- Less Flexibility

Brokerage Firms

A brokerage firm or company is a middleman who connects buyers and sellers to complete a transaction for stock shares, bonds, options, and other financial instruments. Once the transaction has been completed, brokers are compensated in commissions or fees.

Most discount brokerages now offer their customers zero-commission stock trading. The companies make up for this loss of revenue from other sources, including payments from the exchanges for large orders and trading fees for other products like mutual funds and bonds.

In a perfect market in which every party had all the necessary information, brokerage firms would not need to exist. However, that is impossible in a market with many participants making transactions at split-second intervals. The Nasdaq alone has more than 30 million trades per day.

Brokerage companies exist to help their clients match two sides for a trade. They bring together buyers and sellers at the best price possible for each and extract a commission for their service. Full-service brokerages offer additional services, including advice and research on various financial products.

Mortgage Companies

A mortgage company is a specialized financial firm that originates and funds residential or commercial property mortgages. It is often just the originator of a loan; it markets itself to potential borrowers and seeks funding from one of several client financial institutions that provide the capital for the mortgage itself.

A mortgage company is a financial firm that underwrites and issues mortgages to homebuyers, using its own capital to do so. A mortgage company typically only specializes in mortgage products and does not offer other banking services such as checking, investments, or loans for other purposes.

While a mortgage company will originate loans, they may only service your loan or keep it on their balance sheet for a short time. Indeed, a mortgage lender often sells the loan (individually or bundled together with others) to a third-party mortgage servicing institution such as an investment bank, hedge fund, or agency.

People work with mortgage companies because they might offer incentives that buyers might not find at banks. For example, a mortgage company might be more willing to deal with borrowers with less-than-perfect credit or offer loans with no origination fees.

Central Banks

A central bank is a financial institution that is given privileged control over the production and distribution of money and credit for a nation or a group of nations. It is usually responsible for formulating monetary policy and regulating member banks.

Central banks are non-market-based banks. Some are nationalized, and many are not government agencies. The law establishes and protects its privileges even if the government does not legally own a central bank. The critical feature of a central bank is its legal monopoly status, which gives it the privilege to issue banknotes and cash.

Central banks enact monetary policy by easing or tightening the money supply and availability of credit. They also set requirements for the banking industry, such as the amount of cash reserves banks must maintain vis-à-vis their deposits.

A central bank can be a lender to troubled financial institutions and even governments.

Some examples of central banks are the Federal Reserve Bank (U.S.), the Reserve Bank of India (India), and the Bank of England (Britain).

Internet Banks

Online banks are financial institutions that only provide services through a digital medium, but they offer most of the services offered by traditional banks.

Online banks operate exclusively online, meaning they don't operate branches where you can conduct business in person. The best online banks offer low-cost or free banking, plus above-average interest rates on savings accounts and certificates of deposit (CDs).

These banks handle customer service by phone, email, or online chat rather than in person. Prominent online banks in the U.S. include Ally Bank, Discover

Bank, and Synchrony Bank.

Online-only banks might not provide direct automatic teller machine (ATM) access but usually enable customers to use ATMs at other banks and retail stores. They might even reimburse some or all of the ATM fees other financial institutions charge. The savings gained by not maintaining physical branches typically allow online banks to deliver significant savings on banking fees.

Info: Examples of Online banks are Ally Bank and Synchrony Bank.

Savings and Loan Associations

A savings and loan association are a financial institution offering savings accounts and loans.

The most crucial purpose of savings and loan associations is to make mortgage loans on residential property. These organizations, also known as savings associations, building and loan associations, cooperative banks (in New England), and homestead associations (in Louisiana), are the primary source of financial assistance to a large segment of American homeowners. As home-financing institutions, they give primary attention to single-family residences. They are equipped to make loans in this area.

Some of the most essential characteristics of a savings and loan association are:

- It is generally a locally owned and privately managed home financing institution.
- It receives individuals' savings and uses them to make long-term amortized loans to home purchasers.
- It makes loans for constructing, purchasing, repairing, or refinancing houses.
- It is state or federally chartered.

We have seen the different types of Financial Organizations and their characteristics, how they are necessary for individuals, corporates and institutions to manage their finances and serves as the backbone for the economy. The Financial Industry is heavily regulated, and every country has it's own sets of compliances which need to be adhered to. In the next section we will understand the key regulations associated with Financial Services and how they evolved.

Shadow Banking

Shadow banking refers to financial activities and entities that operate outside the traditional banking system, but still provide financial services, such as lending, borrowing, and investing. These activities and entities often lack the same level of regulation and oversight as traditional banks, which can make them riskier and less transparent. Shadow banking can take many forms, including:

1. **Money market funds**: These funds invest in short-term debt securities and offer investors a liquid and low-risk way to invest their money.
2. **Asset-backed securities (ABS)**: These securities are created when banks package and sell mortgages, credit card debt, and other assets to investors.
3. **Private equity and hedge funds**: These investment vehicles pool money from wealthy individuals and institutions to invest in stocks, bonds, and other assets.
4. **Peer-to-peer lending**: This type of lending connects borrowers with investors directly, bypassing traditional banks.
5. **Cryptocurrencies and initial coin offerings (ICOs)**: These digital currencies and fundraising mechanisms operate outside traditional banking systems.

Shadow banking activities could pose systemic risks to the financial system, as they often lack the same level of regulation and oversight as traditional banks.

Financial Services Industry Regulations

A well-functioning Financial System is very important for the economy, businesses, and consumers. Financial activity is inherently risky. As a result of an increasing number of cyberattacks, mainly aimed at the financial industry, various mandatory regulations have been introduced. Regulatory compliance is one of the most successful ways to hold financial services accountable for their security posture. However, it is typically seen as an unneeded burden on security teams.

International regulatory bodies play a crucial role in promoting financial stability, supervising financial institutions, and developing standards for the financial industry. Two prominent examples are the Financial Stability Board (FSB) and the Basel Committee on Banking Supervision (BCBS).

The FSB is an international body that promotes financial stability by coordinating the regulatory response to financial crises. The FSB was established in 2009 in response to the global financial crisis with the objective of identifying and addressing potential vulnerabilities, promoting coordination and cooperation among national regulators and to develop and implement international standards for financial regulation.

BCBS is an international organization that develops global standards for banking supervision and regulation. The BCBS was established in 1974 with the main objectives of promoting the safety and soundness of banks, ensuring the stability of the financial system and implement international standards for banking supervision.

These regulations are a way to ensure that organizations maintain a minimum standard of protection. In the context of building IT solutions for the financial sector, some of the essential Financial Services Regulation requirements to help protect against the cyber-attack are:

General Data Protection Regulation (GDPR)

2016, the EU adopted the General Data Protection Regulation (GDPR). It replaces the 1995 Data Protection Directive, adopted when the Internet was in its infancy. On October 24, 1995, the European Data Protection Directive (Directive 95/46/EC) was adopted for the protection of individuals about the processing of personal data and the free movement of such data) is adopted.

The GDPR reinforces a wide range of existing rights and establishes new ones for individuals. These include the:

- **Right of data portability**: You can quickly receive your data from an organization in a commonly used form and share it with others.
- **Right not to be profiled**: Unless it is necessary by law or a contract, decisions affecting you cannot be made on the sole basis of automated processing.

The European Union's General Data Protection Regulation (EU-GDPR) is a security framework meant to prevent the compromise of citizens' personal data. The GDPR applies to all enterprises that process data about EU individuals, whether manually or through automated processes. It highlights different security guidelines for both data processors and data controllers to secure the entire lifecycle of user data.

GDPR compliance is a mandatory EU requirement for financial services that collect or process personal data from EU residents, regardless of the business's actual location.

Payment Card Industry Data Security Standard (PCI DSS)

PCI DSS was created in 2004 by five major credit card companies: Visa, Mastercard, Discover, JCB, and American Express. The Payment Card Industry Security Standards Council (PCI SSC) developed the guidelines for PCI DSS, which were designed to prevent cybersecurity breaches of sensitive data and reduce the risk of fraud for organizations that handle payment card information.

Credit card firms must comply with PCI DSS to protect the security of credit card transactions. The technical and operational standards that organizations need to follow to secure credit card data provided by cardholders and sent through card processing activities are developed and managed by the PCI Security Standards Council. It should be followed by all organizations that receive or process customer credit card information, including retailers and payment solution providers. PCI DSS compliance requirements are divided into four merchant levels based on the annual volume of credit or debit card transactions processed by a business for both e-commerce and brick-and-mortar transactions.

The six primary goals for PCI DSS are:

- Build and maintain a secure network and systems.
- Protect cardholder data.
- Maintain a vulnerability management program.
- Implement strong access control measures.
- Regularly monitor and test networks.
- Maintain an information security policy.

Sarbanes-Oxley Act (SOX)

The Sarbanes-Oxley Act of 2002 came in response to financial scandals in the early 2000s involving publicly traded companies such as Enron Corporation, Tyco International plc, and WorldCom. The high-profile frauds shook investor confidence in the trustworthiness of corporate financial statements.

The Sarbanes-Oxley (SOX) Act was passed by the United States Congress in 2002 to safeguard investors against financial fraud. Through internal checks, the SOX framework provides recommended security procedures for avoiding fraudulent financial activities.

SOX has expanded into more than merely a framework for assuring the sanctity of financial records. It now contains cybersecurity components to guarantee financial institutions are prepared to deal with frequent cybersecurity threats that could disrupt financial transactions. SOX compliance is essential for all publicly listed businesses, including those in the financial sector.

Gramm-Leach-Bliley Act (GLBA)

Due to the remarkable losses incurred due to 1929's Black Tuesday and Thursday, the Glass-Steagall Act was created to protect bank depositors from additional exposure to risk associated with stock market volatility. As a result, commercial banks were only legally allowed to act as brokers for a few years. Since many regulations have been instituted since the 1930s to protect bank depositors, the GLBA was created to allow these financial industry participants to offer more services.

The Gramm-Leach-Bliley Act of 1999 (GLBA) was passed on November 12, 1999, to update and modernize the financial industry.

The Gramm requires financial institutions–Leach–Bliley Act (GLBA) to secure consumer data and fully disclose all data-sharing practices to clients. They must create security controls to protect client information from any occurrences that risk data integrity and safety under this US statute.

The GLBA includes stringent financial information access rules to reduce the chances of unwanted access and compromise. All businesses selling financial products or services in the United States must comply with the GLBA.

Payment Services Directive (PSD2)

The Payment Services Directive 2 (PSD2) is an upgrade to the original Payment Services Directive (PSD) enacted in 2007. The initial directive established rules and regulations to make cross-border payments as easy, efficient, and secure as 'national' payments within an EU country. However, with the ever-evolving nature of digital payments and the emergence of new payment service providers (PSPs), an update was deemed necessary, leading to the introduction of PSD2 in January 2018.

Since its inception, PSD2 has undergone various iterations to meet the changing landscape of digital payments. A key milestone was the adoption of the Regulatory Technical Standards (RTS) in 2019, which outlined specific requirements for strong customer authentication (SCA) and secure communication. The directive continues to evolve to keep pace with technological advancements, the rise of fintech companies, and changes in customer behavior.

The Payment Services Directive 2 (PSD 2) is a European Union directive that promotes competition in the banking sector. PSD-2 is a financial data security standard developed by the Payment Card Industry Data Security Standard (PCI DSS).

PSD 2 comprises standards for securing online payments, strengthening customer data security, and strong client authentication to ensure that banking transactions in the EU are secure (e.g., multi-factor authentication). The PSD 2 directives apply to all banks and financial institutions in the European Union.

PSD2's significance goes beyond just giving users more control over their data. It also lays the groundwork for the emergence and proliferation of new and innovative payment and accounting services. Through these advancements in financial technology, the directive aims to facilitate a significant increase in consumer protection within the rapidly evolving digital payments landscape.

PSD2 seeks to democratize financial data, promote competition and innovation in the financial technology industry, and bolster consumer rights and protections in the digital sphere.

ISO/IEC 27001

British Standard Institute (BSI) partnered with the International Organization for Standardization (ISO) and the International Electrotechnical Commission (IEC) to develop an internationally recognized standard.

Brief history:

- 1995-1998: BS 7799 Parts 1 and 2 Established in the UK
- 2005: International adoption as ISO 27001 and ISO 27002
- 2007: ISO 27002 updated from the older ISO 17799 version
- 2013 and 2022: Major updates to align with new technologies and cyber threats

ISO/IEC 27001 is a widely accepted worldwide standard for lowering security risks and safeguarding information systems. ISO/IEC 27001 is an internationally recognized set of security policies and processes that provide direction on improving a company's security posture in any industry.

Financial institutions that want to demonstrate their exceptional cybersecurity procedures to stakeholders should pursue ISO/IEC 27001 accreditation, given its image as an internationally recognized benchmark for cyber-attack resilience. Although ISO 27001 is not mandatory in most countries, it is highly recommended for businesses in the financial services sector due to the framework's superior protection of sensitive data.

The list of regulations is huge and ever evolving, and it is sometimes overwhelming for the organizations to ensure adherence to all the regulations and compliances. Most of the Financial institutes have a separate department dedicated to this purpose, generally called "Security, Risk and Compliances".

However, these regulations are imperative for a well-functioning Financial System which directly impacts the economy, businesses, and consumers.

As we know, financial sector has seen immense growth in the last few decades riding on the globalization and technology advancements. In the next section, we will discuss about the Fintech Revolution, its history and fintech products.

Regulations for Use of Artificial Intelligence (AI) in Finance Industry

The European Union (EU) and United States (US) have introduced regulations to ensure the responsible development and use of AI in the financial industry. These regulations focus on ensuring transparency, explainability, accountability, security, and governance. While there are differences between the two regulatory frameworks, they share a common goal of promoting the safe and efficient use of AI in the financial sector.

European Union (EU):

1. **Artificial Intelligence Act (AIA)**: The EU introduced the AIA in April 2021, which aims to regulate the development, deployment, and use of AI systems in various sectors, including finance. The AIA focuses on ensuring AI systems are transparent, explainable, and unbiased.
2. **Financial Technology (FinTech) Regulation**: The EU's FinTech Regulation, introduced in 2018, aims to regulate the use of AI and other technologies in the financial sector. The regulation focuses on ensuring the security, integrity, and stability of financial markets.

United States (US):

1. **Federal Reserve's Supervisory Guidance**: In 2020, the Federal Reserve issued supervisory guidance on the use of AI and machine learning in banking, focusing on ensuring the safety and soundness of financial institutions.
2. **Commodity Futures Trading Commission (CFTC) Regulations**: The CFTC has issued regulations on the use of AI and other technologies in derivatives trading, emphasizing the need for transparency, accountability, and risk management.

Securing Mobile Apps Transactions for Banking

Most of the banks are now using Mobile Apps to satisfy the customer urge for quick transactions, increase convenience and have a competitive edge. The mobile apps need enhanced security measures to safeguard the customers from frauds. Biometry and facial technologies have become increasingly popular in the financial sector, particularly in mobile banking apps, to enhance security and provide a more seamless user experience.

Biometry: Biometric authentication involves the use of unique physical characteristics, such as fingerprints, iris scans, or facial recognition, to verify an individual's identity. In the context of mobile banking apps, biometric authentication can be used to:

1. **Replace traditional login credentials**: Instead of entering passwords or PINs, users can use their biometric data to authenticate themselves.
2. **Enhance transaction security**: Biometric authentication can provide an additional layer of security by requiring users to verify their identity before completing transactions.
3. **Simplify login processes**: Biometric authentication can reduce the need for users to remember complex passwords or PINs.

Facial Technologies: Facial recognition technology uses facial features, such as the shape of the eyes, nose, and mouth, to identify an individual. In mobile banking apps, facial recognition can be used for:

1. **Face-based authentication**: Users can use their facial features to authenticate themselves, eliminating the need for passwords or PINs.
2. **Biometric verification**: Facial recognition can be used to verify the identity of users, ensuring that transactions are authorized by the account holder.

Let's understand how Biometry and Facial Technologies Work Together. Many mobile banking apps now integrate biometric and facial technologies to provide a more secure and convenient experience. Some examples include :

1. **Initial Enrollment**: Users enroll their biometric data, such as fingerprints or facial features, during the app's initial setup process.
2. **Authentication**: When users open the app, they are prompted to authenticate themselves using their biometric data (e.g., fingerprint scan or facial recognition).
3. **Transaction Verification**: Before completing a transaction, users are required to verify their identity using their biometric data again.
4. **Secure Transactions**: Once authenticated, users can access their accounts and complete transactions securely, knowing that their identity is verified.

The use of biometry and facial technologies in mobile banking apps offers several benefits, including:

1. Enhanced Security: Biometric and facial technologies provide an additional layer of security, making it more difficult for hackers to access users' accounts.

2. Convenience: Users no longer need to remember complex passwords or PINs, making the login process simpler and faster.

3. User Experience: Biometric and facial technologies provide a seamless and intuitive experience, allowing users to focus on their financial transactions rather than complex authentication processes.

While biometry and facial technologies offer many benefits, there are also some challenges and considerations associated with it, like:

1. **Accuracy**: Biometric and facial recognition technologies are not foolproof and can be affected by various factors, such as lighting conditions, facial hair, or makeup.
2. **Data Privacy**: Users' biometric and facial data must be stored securely and handled in compliance with data protection regulations.
3. **Regulation**: The use of biometric and facial technologies in financial services is subject to regulatory oversight, and banks and financial institutions must ensure compliance with relevant laws and guidelines.

In conclusion, biometry and facial technologies have revolutionized the way we interact with mobile banking apps, providing a more secure, convenient, and seamless experience. However, it's essential to address the challenges and considerations associated with their use to ensure the integrity and security of financial transactions.

We have looked at the overview of financial sector, the types of financial organizations, the regulatory requirements and how to address the need of enhanced security for the mobile applications. In the next section, we will read about the Fintech revolution and the types of fintech products available in the market.

Fintech Revolution

Financial technology (better known as fintech) is a term for new technology that seeks to improve and automate the delivery and use of financial services. Fintech encompasses many applications, such as mobile banking, open banking, digital payments, peer-to-peer lending, blockchain-based cryptocurrencies, robo-advisors, and payment processing.

Fintech leverages advancements in data analytics, artificial intelligence, and secure online platforms to streamline financial transactions, reduce costs, and improve accessibility for consumers and businesses. Fintech has revolutionized finance, particularly in the consumer sphere, where access to financial services and payment methods has increased sharply.

Additionally, Decentralized Finance (DeFi) and Central Bank Digital Currencies

(CBDCs) are two other concepts that are transforming the financial ecosystem. While DeFi provides a decentralized, open-source alternative to traditional financial services, CBDCs offer a centralized, fiat-backed digital currency. The intersection of these two concepts will likely lead to increased competition, improved financial inclusion, and enhanced efficiency in the financial sector.

Fintech companies often collaborate with traditional financial institutions, regulatory bodies, and other stakeholders to ensure compliance with financial regulations & industry standards.

A Brief History of FinTech

While fintech seems like a recent series of technological breakthroughs, the basic concept has existed for some time. Early credit cards in the 1950s generally represent the first fintech products available to the public. They eliminated the need for consumers to carry physical currency in their day-to-day lives.

From there, fintech evolved to include bank mainframes and online stock trading services. In 1998, PayPal was founded, representing one of the first fintech companies to operate primarily on the Internet—a breakthrough that has been further revolutionized by mobile technology, social media, and data encryption. This fintech revolution has led to the mobile payment apps, blockchain networks, and social media-housed payment options we regularly use today.

Types of Fintech products

Fintech products are important for the modern economy as they bring in significant benefits for both the consumers and businesses. While consumers get more personalization, convenience and competitive offerings, businesses get the advantages of Cost Effectiveness, Efficiency and Accessibility.

By leveraging the new technologies, fintech companies can further improve the efficiency, security, and customer experience of their products and services, ultimately driving innovation and growth in the financial industry. For e.g. Artificial Intelligence (AI) and Machine Learning (ML) can help fintech companies analyze large amounts of data to identify patterns, predict customer behavior, and make more accurate risk assessments. This can lead to improved decision-making, fraud detection, and personalized customer experiences.

Some of the top fintech products are mentioned below:

Payment & Money Transfer Services

This refers to the electronic transfer of funds from one entity to another. It can be between individuals or businesses:

- **Mobile payment apps**—Mobile payment, also referred to as mobile money, mobile money transfer, or mobile wallet, is any of various payment processing services operated under financial regulations and performed from or via a mobile device, such as Google Pay, Apple Pay, PayPal, etc.
- **Digital wallets**—A digital wallet (or electronic wallet) is a financial transaction application that runs on any connected device. It securely stores your payment information and passwords in the cloud. Digital wallets may be accessible from a computer or mobile device, such as Google Wallet, Apple Pay, or Walmart Pay.
- **Peer-to-peer (P2P) payment platforms** - A peer-to-peer service is a platform that directly connects parties in a transaction without a third-party intermediary. They leverage technology to overcome the transaction costs of trust, enforcement, and information asymmetries traditionally addressed by using trusted third parties. Peer-to-peer platforms offer services such as payment processing, information about buyers and sellers, and quality assurance to their users. For e.g., Cash App, Zelle, etc.

Online Lending & Crowdfunding

Crowd funding is the way to raise money to finance projects or businesses. Online lending or crowd funding is used to collect money from many people via online platforms.:

- **Peer-to-peer lending platforms** - Peer-to-peer (P2P) lending is a form of financial technology that allows people to lend or borrow money from one another without going through a bank. Examples include Faircent and Upstart.
- **Online personal and business loans**—These apps provide instant personal and business loans online with quick approvals and flexible repayment options. For e.g. PaySense, Home Credit, LendingKart etc
- **Crowdfunding platforms**—Crowdfunding platforms facilitate and help raise funds for your business idea, nonprofit cause, or personal needs easily. Examples are MightyCause, StartEngine, and GoFundMe.

Robo Advisors

Robo-advisors are financial advisers that provide digital financial advice and investment management based on mathematical rules or algorithms. Each robo-advisor is different, but they tend to work in similar fashion:

- **Automated investment platforms** – Online investing platform that employs software algorithms to create and manage investment portfolios. E.g. M1Finance
- **Algorithm-driven portfolio management**—Clients and others can link their investment accounts or manually input them for a 360-degree view and analysis of their finances, E.g., WealthFront.
- **Goal-based financial planning**—Users can integrate their robo-advisor account with their external accounts through Path for high-level goal planning. The calculators embedded within the Path digital financial planner help with retirement, homeownership, and college planning, as well as the finances involved in taking a break from work. E.g., VanGaurd.

Insurtech

Innovative technologies like Artificial Intelligence, Machine Learning, BlockChain etc. are being used by Insurtech to improve and automate the traditional insurance sector. :

- **Insurance comparison websites** - Insurtech refers to technological innovations designed to find cost savings and efficiency based on the current insurance industry model. Compare Insurance Policies from leading insurance providers in the country to help you select the best. E.g. PolicyX
- **Digital insurance underwriting & claims processing** - Digital claims processing technology is a type of InsurTech that empowers adjusters and agents to automate manual tasks, sift through large data sets and paperwork, and provide policyholders with a fast and straightforward customer experience. E.g. DigitalEdge Insurance Platform
- **Telematics-based auto insurance** – It is an app-based telematics for an auto insurance program that provides rewards for safe driving, emergency/crash assistance, and other services beyond monitoring driving behavior (e.g., Progressive Snapshot)

Digital Banking

Digital Banking refers to accessing the banking services online via internet. Fintech has taken it a step ahead and now we also have banks which are completely online with no physical buildings at all.

- **Neobanks** – Bank that operates exclusively using online banking. E.g., Chime.
- **Mobile banking apps** - Mobile banking is a service a bank provides that allows its customers to conduct financial transactions remotely using a mobile device such as a smartphone or tablet.

- **Virtual cards and Banking-as-a-Service (BaaS) Platforms**—BaaS is an end-to-end model that allows digital banks and other third parties to connect with banks' systems directly via APIs so they can build banking offerings on top of the providers' regulated infrastructure and unlock the open banking opportunity reshaping the global financial services landscape.

Blockchain and Cryptocurrency

Cryptocurrencies like Bitcoin and Ethereum are digital means of payment and make use of the technology called the blockchain:

- **Cryptocurrency exchanges** - Cryptocurrency exchanges operate similarly to other central exchanges, such as traditional online brokerages. They offer the tools to research, trade, and invest in Bitcoin and other cryptocurrencies. E.g. Kraken, CoinBase.
- **Blockchain-based intelligent contracts**—Smart contracts are digital contracts stored on a blockchain that are automatically executed when predetermined terms and conditions are met.
- **Decentralized finance (DeFi) applications** - DeFi uses emerging technology to remove third parties and centralized institutions from financial transactions. The components of DeFi are cryptocurrencies, blockchain technology, and software that allow people to transact financially with each other. E.g. UniSwap

Regtech

RegTech, short for Regulatory Technology, refers to the use of technology to improve the way regulatory requirements are met, managed, and monitored. It involves the development and implementation of innovative solutions to help organizations comply with regulatory requirements, reduce regulatory risk, and enhance transparency and accountability.

RegTech solutions can be applied across various industries, including financial services, healthcare, energy, and more. Some common examples of RegTech include:

- **Know-Your-Customer (KYC) and Anti-Money Laundering (AML) solutions**: These technologies help organizations verify customer identities and detect suspicious transactions to prevent financial crimes. KYC and AML solutions provide quality data on millions of individuals and entities, enabling risk-based decisions with the utmost confidence. E.g. ComplyAdvantage.
- **Compliance monitoring and reporting tools**: RegTech platforms can help

organizations track and report compliance with regulatory requirements, reducing the risk of non-compliance and potential fines. E.g. OneTrust

- OneTrust is a software platform that helps organizations manage and protect sensitive data, ensure compliance with data protection regulations, and maintain transparency with data subjects. It offers a range of products and services that cater to the needs of businesses, government agencies, and other organizations that handle personal data.
- **Risk management and assessment platforms**: RegTech solutions can help organizations identify, assess, and mitigate risks, ensuring they follow the regulatory requirements. Fraud Risk Management tools are readily available to detect & prevent fraud & devise effective risk assessment strategies. E.g. Signifyd
- **Regulatory reporting and filing tools**: These technologies simplify the process of submitting regulatory reports and filings, reducing the risk of errors and delays.
- **Audit and compliance management platforms**: RegTech solutions can help organizations manage audits and compliance activities, ensuring that they follow regulatory requirements.

The benefits of RegTech include:

- **Cost savings**: RegTech solutions can help organizations reduce the costs associated with compliance, such as manual processing and paper-based reporting.
- **Increased efficiency**: RegTech platforms can automate many compliance tasks, freeing up resources for more strategic activities.
- **Improved accuracy**: RegTech solutions can help reduce errors and inaccuracies associated with manual compliance processes.
- **Enhanced transparency**: RegTech platforms can provide real-time visibility into compliance activities, ensuring transparency and accountability.
- **Better risk management**: RegTech solutions can help organizations identify and mitigate risks, reducing the risk of regulatory non-compliance.

The use of new technologies can further enhance the RegTech to a large Extent, as follows:

- **Artificial Intelligence (AI) and Machine Learning (ML)**: AI and ML can be used to analyze large amounts of data, identify patterns, and detect anomalies in regulatory compliance. This can help automate manual tasks, reduce errors, and improve the accuracy of compliance monitoring. For example, AI-powered chatbots can be used to provide real-time compliance guidance to employees
- **Blockchain**: Blockchain technology can be used to create a secure, transparent, and tamper-proof record of regulatory compliance. This can help ensure that data is accurate, secure, and accessible, and can reduce the risk of fraud and non-compliance.
- **Cloud Computing**: Cloud computing can provide RegTech solutions with

scalable and flexible infrastructure, allowing them to process large amounts of data and scale quickly to meet changing regulatory requirements.

- **Internet of Things (IoT)**: IoT devices can be used to collect and transmit data in real-time, allowing RegTech solutions to monitor and analyze compliance in real-time. This can help detect and prevent non-compliance before it occurs.
- **Natural Language Processing (NLP)** can be used to analyze and interpret regulatory texts, making it easier to understand complex regulations and identify compliance risks. Predictive Analytics: Predictive analytics can be used to analyze historical data and predict future compliance risks, allowing RegTech solutions to proactively identify and mitigate potential compliance issues.
- **Quantum Computing**: Quantum computing can be used to solve complex mathematical problems and optimize compliance processes, allowing RegTech solutions to process large amounts of data quickly and accurately.
- **Cybersecurity**: Cybersecurity solutions can be integrated with RegTech solutions to ensure that sensitive data is protected and that compliance processes are secure.

Overall, the integration of new technologies with RegTech solutions can help improve the efficiency, accuracy, and effectiveness of regulatory compliance, reducing the risk of non-compliance and improving the overall governance and risk management of an organization.

Personal Finance Management

There are multiple Fintech products to help the consumers with personal finance management. Some examples are:

- **Budgeting and expense-tracking apps**—An expense tracker app is an investment tracking and analysis tool that monitors and categorizes expenses across different bank and investment accounts and credit cards. Some of these apps also offer budgeting tools, credit monitoring, mileage tracking, receipt keeping, and advice to grow your net worth, e.g., QuickBooks and Evelance.
- **Financial literacy & education platforms** – Apps to provide knowledge of and ability to use financial skills. E.g. Zogo, RoosterMoney

In this section, we looked at some of the examples of Fintech products and the impact they are having on the Financial Industry. There is no looking back and technology is expected to bring many more positive disruptions.

Conclusion

Understanding the financial services landscape is crucial for anyone looking to navigate the complexities of modern economies. In this chapter, we explored this sector's various components, functions, and interactions, diving insights into how financial services drive economic activity, manage risks, and contribute to overall economic well-being.

In the next chapter, we will explore and discuss the evolution of the banking industry.

References

https://omnicard.in/blogs/fintech-261023
https://bootcamp.cvn.columbia.edu/blog/what-is-fintech/
https://www.appknox.com/blog/cybersecurity-regulations-in-the-financial-industry
https://www.edps.europa.eu/data-protection/data-protection/
https://www.techtarget.com/searchsecurity/definition/
https://27kay.com/iso-27001-a-brief-history-of-the-information-security-standard
https://www.kiteworks.com/risk-compliance-glossary/psd2/
https://www.theforage.com/blog/careers/difference-between-retail-commercial-banking
https://corporatefinanceinstitute.com/resources/career/investment-banking-overview/
https://www.investopedia.com/
https://en.wikipedia.org/wiki/

Notes

Date:

Chapter 3
Evolution of Banking Industry

In this chapter we will take a sneak peek into the past and get a glimpse of how the Banking Industry has evolved over time. We will see how the currencies were originated and where were they stored to keep them secured. The chapter will cover the history of banking, the adaptation of IT in Banking and the significance of Mobile banking revolution. Globalization, Information Technology and Mobile Banking are the key disruptors in the Banking industry and will be a constant topic of discussion throughout the book.

In this chapter we will discuss:

- Evolution of Banking as an Industry
- Understanding the History of Banking
- Adaptation of Technology in Banking

Evolution of Banking as an Industry

Banking is probably one of the oldest businesses in the world and is an integral part of any society. Economies thrive and flourishes on the efficient functioning of the Banking industry. Banks, as we see today, have gone through numerous evolutions since it's inception. Thousands of years ago, when the currencies were not invented, banking was primarily done using the barter system of exchanging goods for goods. People used to trade grains and other necessary items. Farmers would store the grains in the grain banks and take them out periodically for trading till the time next crop is harvested.

The commodity-based trading became un-manageable owing to the logistics involved, and an alternative approach was sought. It is believed that the first coin came into existence in 5th or 6th century. The coins of various shapes and sizes were minted to represent the denomination for the value they hold. Coins had to be kept safe and religious temples served as a secure place for storing them. Hence, temples served as the first banks during the ancient times. The priests maintained the record of the transactions, i.e. coins deposited and being taken out, which served as the initial form of book-keeping.

With the spread of civilization, private depositors and money lenders came into existence. The coins evolved into centralized medium of exchange, also known as currency. As currency developed, so did banking and the initial seeds of establishing banking as an industry were sown.

In the next section, we will look at the history of banking and how it evolved from its origin to the current structure.

Understanding the History of Banking

Looking at the current banking system, we may not realize how much it has evolved since its inception. Currency was part of our systems even before the banks were developed.

The figure below shows the emergence of banks from the initial 2000 BCE, when barter system was used in local communities, to the Modern Era of Global Digital Banking. The banking industry has gone through a lot of ups and downs, including the financial crises and bank panics. All this has contributed towards the modern banking and strict regulations surrounding it. In this section, we will cover the significant milestones that have shaped the industry.

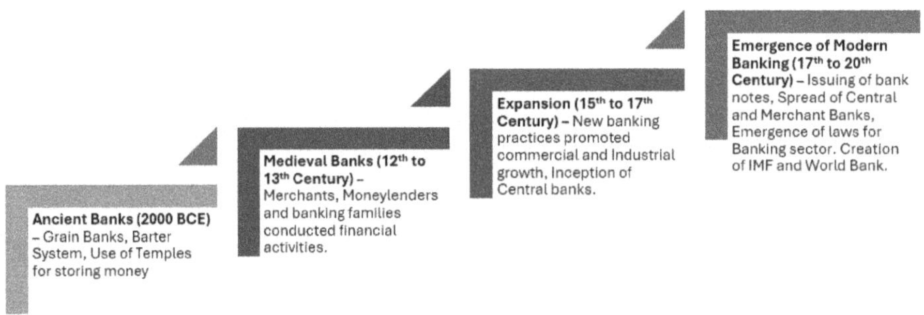

Figure 3.1: History of Banking

Ancient Banks

The first bank, a cornerstone of early communities, emerged around **2000 BCE** in the ancient empires of Egypt, Assyria, India, and Sumeria. These banks facilitated the exchange of goods and the measurement of value through various methods, including grain banks, barter systems, and metal weights. The barter system was a testament to the early communities' resourcefulness and cooperation.

As trade expanded, the need for a secure store of value became apparent. This led to the minting of coins and the emergence of ancient banks. These early banks, with their unwavering commitment to security, laid the foundation for the modern banking system.

Medieval Banks (12th to 13th Century)

The Romans, expert builders and administrators, extricated banking from the temples and formalized it within distinct buildings. Banking activities expanded with the rise of trade and commerce. Merchants, moneylenders, and early banking families such as the Medici in Italy established banking institutions and conducted financial transactions, including money lending, investments, etc.

Expansion (15th to 17th Century)

By the end of the 16th century and during the 17th century, new banking practices had promoted commercial and industrial growth. It was primarily because of the safe and convenient means of payment and easily available money for the commercial needs.

By the end of the 17th century, banking was also becoming essential for the funding requirements of the combative European states. This led to government regulations and the first central banks.

Emergence Of Modern Banking (17th to 20th Century)

In 1695, the Bank of England became one of the first banks to issue banknotes. Initially, these were hand-written and issued on deposit or as a loan and promised to pay the bearer the note's value on demand. By 1745, standardized printed notes were being issued.

The 18th century witnessed a significant expansion in the services offered by banks. The number of banks increased during the Industrial Revolution, and this period saw the emergence of new types of financial activities that broadened the scope of banking. The new 'merchant banks' played a crucial role in facilitating trade growth.

In the 19th century, banks began establishing branch networks to serve customers across different geographical locations. The spread of railways and telegraph communication further facilitated the growth and coordination of banking operations. Central banks were established in many European countries during the 19th century.

In 1913, the U.S. government formed the Federal Reserve Bank (the Fed). When World War I broke out, the United States became a global lender, and by the end of the war, it had replaced London as the center of the financial world. The government insisted that all debtor nations pay back their war loans before any American institution would extend them further credit.

This slowed down world trade. The already-slow world economy was further damaged when the stock market crashed on "Black Tuesday" in 1929. The Fed could not contain the damage, leading to 9,000 bank failures from 1929 to 1933.

New laws emerged to salvage the banking sector and restore consumer confidence. Many countries significantly increased financial regulation. During the post-Second World War period, two organizations were created: the International Monetary Fund (IMF) and the World Bank.

Around the mid-1990s, the possibility of using technology in retail banking was realized. In 1959, banks agreed on a standard for machine-readable characters (MICR), which led to the first automated reader-sorter machines. In the 1960s, the first automated teller machines (ATM) or cash machines were developed, and the first machines started to appear by the end of the decade.

Banks started to invest in computer technology to automate much of the manual processing, which began a shift by banks from large clerical staff to new automated systems.

The 'Modern Era' of banking, ushered in by globalization, has seen a rapid expansion of banking services. Technology has played a pivotal role in this, enabling banks to reach a large part of the market in a relatively short period. This exponential growth, fueled by technology, has made banking more efficient and accessible, leading to the creation of new models, products, services, and even organizations.

Example – Evolution of Barclays Bank

Let's look at one real life example of "Barclays Bank" which has gone through the evolution cycle in Banking. Barclays Bank is one of the oldest banks in the UK. It was founded in 1690 and is now one of the big four banks that have the largest market share of UK customers. The bank was founded by John Freame and Thomas Gould, who were goldsmiths in the city of London. At that time goldsmiths acted as bankers giving out loans to businesses and merchants.

The company's early focus was on providing financial services to merchants and traders. In 1736, the bank's name was changed to Freame & Gould.

Expansion and Growth (1800s-1900s)

In 1825, Freame & Gould merged with Barclay & Co., a rival bank, and the company's name was changed to Barclay & Freame. The bank expanded its operations, opening branches in London and the countryside. In 1896, the bank's name was changed to Barclays Bank Limited.

The 20th Century (1900s-1990s)

During the 20th century, Barclays Bank continued to grow and expand globally. Some notable milestones include:

- The establishment of Barclays Bank D.C.O. (Domestic and Colonial Overseas) in 1925, which focused on international banking and investments.
- The launch of the first debit card, the Barclays Bankcard, in 1966.
- The introduction of the first credit card, the Barclaycard, in 1967.
- The acquisition of the British Bank of the Middle East in 1959, which expanded Barclays' presence in the Middle East.
- The merger with National Westminster Bank in 1970, creating one of the largest banks in the world.

Modernization and Digitalization (1990s-present)

In the 1990s and 2000s, Barclays Bank invested heavily in technology and digitalization. Some notable developments include:

- The launch of the first online banking service in 1995.
- The introduction of mobile banking services in 2007.
- The acquisition of the Woolwich bank in 2000, which expanded Barclays' presence in the UK mortgage market.
- The merger with Absa Group in 2005, creating a major banking presence in Africa.
- The acquisition of the US-based bank, Lehman Brothers, in 2008, which expanded Barclays' presence in the US financial markets.

Recent Developments

In recent years, Barclays Bank has continued to evolve and adapt to changing market conditions. Some notable developments include:

- The launch of the Barclays app in 2013, which allows customers to manage their accounts and make transactions on-the-go.
- The introduction of contactless payment technology in 2014.
- The acquisition of the US-based financial technology company, BlueIQ, in 2015.
- The launch of the Barclays Bankcard, a contactless credit card, in 2016.
- The introduction of the Barclays Debit Card, a digital-only debit card, in 2020.

Throughout its history, Barclays Bank has remained committed to providing high-quality financial services to its customers. Today, the bank is a global financial institution with operations in over 40 countries and a diverse range of products and services catering to individuals, businesses, and governments worldwide.

In this section we looked at the evolution of banking over the years, along with a real-life example of Barclays Bank evolution. In the next section, we will understand more about the evolution of technology in the Banking industry.

Adaptation of Technology in Banking

For decades, the banking sector has maintained its position at the forefront of modern technological advancement. Looking back at how the industry has rapidly evolved over the centuries, the most notable beginning was in **1950**.

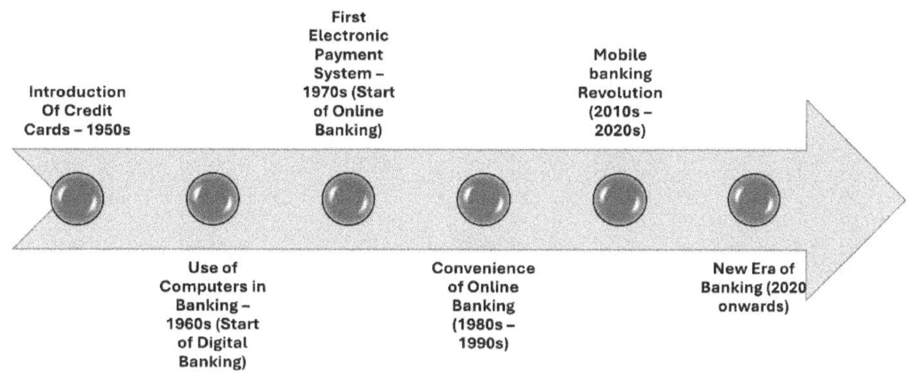

Figure 3.2: Adaptation of Technology in Banking

Introduction of credit cards – 1950s

First introduced by the Diners Club, a credit card was deemed the first notable payment solution that could be used at several different establishments. This invention radically altered how people perceive finances, as they no longer need to carry cash for every purchase.

Use of Computers in Banking – 1960s

Computers were introduced in banking in the 1960s when the then-Bank of New South Wales purchased its first computer for £1 million.

This sparked the first digital banking revolution. The first forms of digital banking started in the 1960s when banks began using mainframe computers to automate banking functions such as check processing and customer account management.

Convenience of Online Banking

The term 'online' became popular in the late 1980s and referred to using a terminal, keyboard, and TV or monitor to access the banking system over a phone line.

Online banking portals were developed due to increased internet use in the 1990s and 2000s. Banks started creating online portals to enable consumers to see account balances, transfer money, and pay bills from their home computers.

Late in the 1990s, consumers were introduced to PayPal, a P2P money service that enabled wireless transfers. These services made it more convenient for people to pay for services wirelessly.

The Mobile Banking Revolution

The enhanced use of smartphones in the late 2000s and early 2010s led to the emergence of mobile banking. Banks began offering mobile apps that allowed customers to access their accounts from their smartphones, enabling them to check account balances, transfer funds, and pay bills on the go.

In 2011, Google introduced Google Wallet, a mobile payment technology that rivals credit cards. For the first time, people could use their phones to make purchases. This provided a new level of freedom, taking technology in the financial industry to a new level. Similarly, in 2014, Apple launched Apple Pay.

In 2015, the EMV chip technology became a standard among card issuers. The "EMV chips make cards far more secure because the information transmitted is encrypted and tokenized." It also adds more security, which is "critical as payments become more integrated."

The New Era of Banking

With growing internet penetration and digitalization, banking sectors have made innovative shifts to address the consumer's needs. By delivering banking services over the Internet, banks have managed to advance their offerings and attract a large consumer base. In today's dynamic banking landscape, digital transformation is taking center stage, driven by the rising demand for seamless and personalized customer experiences.

Banking applications increasingly opt for cloud-based technologies to revamp their processes and benefit from scalability and flexibility. Cloud providers have effectively communicated their ability to deliver dependable solutions, influencing banks to adapt to stay competitive. The cloud also gives banks the potential to synchronize their organizations, break down operational silos, and gain advanced analytics to generate integrated insights

In the last decade, the financial industry has seen many innovative breakthroughs that have transformed its landscape.

Using AI and process automation has allowed banks to increase value by experiencing end-to-end automation, a higher customer lifetime, and lowered operation costs. With AI adoptions come several other new technologies that banks are embracing, such as Robotic Process Automation (RPA), Machine Learning (ML), Deep Learning (DL), Neural Networks, an adaptation of Chatbots, Computer Vision, and Natural Language Processing (NLP). We will cover these more in the chapter "Peak into the Future."

As technology advances rapidly, the banking industry has quickly adopted new tools and techniques to enhance the customer experience, increase efficiency, and improve security. Cloud-based services, particularly cloud-native offerings and composable banking, are recognized as essential enablers in satisfying these requirements.

Financial institutions increasingly opt for cloud-based technologies to revamp their processes and benefit from scalability and flexibility. Cloud providers have effectively communicated their ability to deliver dependable solutions, influencing banks to adapt to stay competitive. The cloud also gives banks the potential to synchronize their organizations, break down operational silos, and gain advanced analytics to generate integrated insights.

Impact of BigTech and FinTech

Some of the other disruptive technologies witnessed by banking and non-banking entities are BigTech and Fintech. BigTech refers to a group of large technology companies that have significant influence and control over the global technology industry and work in multiple sectors. These companies are often characterized by their massive scale, global reach, and significant market value.

Fintech, short for Financial Technology, encompasses a wide range of innovations and startups that aim to improve and automate financial services, processes, and systems. Fintech companies use technology to provide innovative financial products, services, and platforms that cater to various financial needs.

As the financial sector prepares for the next digital revolution, banks face even more challenging competition with the emergence of competitors from within and outside the field (fintech and start-ups included). This has changed the financial landscape, in which tech-savvy banking customers have gained more control over their financial transactions, shifting customer behavior trends.

One such example is the adaptation of **eKYC** (Electronic Know Your Customer) for electronic verification process to verify the identity of an individual or organization. It is a significant offering which has helped banks reduce financial crimes and money laundering through accurate facial identification and biometric authentication. This technology essentially assisted banks in realizing their customer acquisition processes in remote locations, as it required no physical administration. This technology also minimizes the risks of identity falsification and phishing, ensuring zero error margins in the customer identification stage.

The step-by-step explanation of how eKYC works is as follows:

1. **Data Collection**: The individual or organization provides their personal details, such as name, date of birth, address, and other relevant information.
2. **Biometric Authentication**: The individual provides their biometric data, such as fingerprints, facial recognition, or iris scans, to verify their identity.
3. **Document Verification**: The individual provides digital copies of their identification documents to verify their identity.
4. **Data Verification and Validation**: The eKYC system matches the provided data with the data stored in government databases or other trusted sources to verify the individual's identity. If the data matches, the individual's identity is confirmed.
5. **Authentication**: The individual is authenticated, and their identity is verified. This authentication is usually done through a unique identifier, such as a password or PIN.
6. **Data Storage**: The verified identity data is stored in a secure database, which can be accessed by authorized parties.

Adaptation of Banking API

The diverse competition and emphasis on customer-centric systems also brought the adoption of application programming interfaces (APIs) by banks, as the organizations can utilize them to link their product offerings, services, customers, and value providers in one place. Banking APIs are a set of predefined rules that enable financial institutions to share their financial data and services with other organizations, such as fintech companies, through a standardized interface. These APIs allow developers to integrate banking services into their applications, enabling a wide range of innovative financial products and services.

Use of Banking APIs promotes increased competition and efficiency along with improved customer experience. Banking APIs create new revenue streams for financial institutions by enabling them to offer value-added services to customers. Use of banking APIs also leads to enhanced transparency by providing customers with access to their financial data and enabling them to make informed decisions.

Some of the key characteristics of the Banking APIs are :

1. **Standardized interface**: Banking APIs provide a standardized interface for accessing and manipulating financial data, making it easier for developers to integrate banking services into their applications.
2. **Secure**: Banking APIs are designed to be highly secure, with robust authentication and authorization mechanisms to protect sensitive financial data.
3. **Real-time access**: Banking APIs provide real-time access to financial data, enabling developers to build applications that require up-to-date information.
4. **Scalable**: Banking APIs are designed to handle high volumes of traffic and data, making them suitable for large-scale applications.

Let's look at some of the real life uses cases for Banking APIs :

1. **Payment initiation**: Allowing customers to initiate payments from other banks.
2. Account information services: Providing customers with access to their account information.
3. **Transaction monitoring**: Tracking transactions and detecting fraudulent activity.
4. **Data aggregation**: Combining account data from multiple banks into a single view.
5. **Personal finance management**: Enabling customers to manage their finances through a single application.
6. **Investment management**: Enabling customers to invest in stocks, bonds, and other financial instruments through a single application.
7. **Lending platforms**: Enabling customers to borrow money from multiple lenders through a single application.

There is no doubt that the future of banking will continue to leverage APIs, data analytics, cloud, and its associated innovations to allow financial institutes and banks to cater to consumers' needs further.

Unlocking Financial Innovation through Open Banking

Open Banking is a financial services revolution that allows customers to share their financial data with third-party providers, such as fintech companies, through secure APIs (Application Programming Interfaces). This enables a more open and competitive financial ecosystem, where customers can access a wider range of financial products and services.

In 2018, the European Union introduced the Second Payment Services Directive (PSD2), which mandated that banks open their customer data to third-party providers. This gave birth to Open Banking. Since then, many countries have followed suit, including the United States, Australia, and the United Kingdom.

Open Banking can help Fintechs in many ways, like :

1. **Access to customer data**: Fintechs can access customers' financial data, such as transaction history, account balances, and payment details, to offer personalized financial services and products.
2. **Increased competition**: Open Banking levels the playing field, allowing fintechs to compete with traditional banks and offer innovative financial solutions that cater to customers' evolving needs.
3. **Improved customer experience**: Fintechs can develop seamless, integrated financial products and services that simplify the customer experience, reducing friction and increasing adoption.
4. **Reduced costs**: By accessing customer data through APIs, fintechs can reduce the need for manual data collection, which saves time and resources.
5. **New business models**: Open Banking enables fintechs to create new business models, such as account aggregation, budgeting tools, and investment platforms, that offer customers more flexibility and control over their financial lives.
6. **Customer security**: Open Banking follows strict security guidelines, ensuring that customer data is protected and secure, which builds trust with customers and regulators.

Some examples of FinTechs that have benefited from Open Banking include:

- Account aggregation platforms, such as Plaid and Stripe, which allow customers to link their bank accounts and track their financial activity in one place.
- Budgeting and expense tracking apps, such as Mint and Personal Capital, which can access customers' financial data to provide personalized financial advice.
- Investment platforms, such as Robinhood and Stash, which use Open Banking to allow customers to invest in stocks, ETFs, and other financial products.

In summary, Open Banking has unlocked new opportunities for fintechs to innovate, compete, and provide customers with more personalized and convenient financial services.

Security and Data Breaches

However, with enhanced flexibility comes increased responsibility and risks.

With banks now accessible over the Internet, the importance of securing customer data and financial information becomes very important, without which online banking cannot operate. Banks must set up the required security processes to reduce the risk of unauthorized access to a customer's records.

Let's look at some of the data breach incidents that highlight the importance of robust security measures and regular testing:

1. **First American Financial's 2019 Data Breach:** In 2019, First American Financial, an insurance company, reported a data breach affecting over 885,000 customers. Hackers gained access to customers' sensitive information, including Social Security numbers, addresses, and financial data. First American had to reach a $1 million settlement with the New York Department for this massive data breach.

2. **Capital One's 2019 Data Breach:** In 2019, Capital One reported one of the largest data breaches impacting the privacy and security of personal information of over a 100 million individuals. Hackers gained access to customers' personal and financial information, including Social Security numbers, addresses, and account numbers.

3. **Target's 2013 Data Breach:** Target, a major American retailer, experienced a massive data breach in 2013. This was one of the biggest security breaches in history. Target was required to pay an $18.5 million settlement after hackers stole 40 million credit and debit records.

4. **JPMorgan Chase's 2014 Data Breach:** was a cyberattack against the American that compromised data associated with over 83 million accounts—76 million households and 7 million small businesses. The data breach is considered one of the most serious intrusions into an American corporation's information system.

This shows how crucial it is for banks and financial institutions to prioritize their customers' data security and take proactive steps to protect against future breaches.

Fintech companies are leveraging various technologies to enhance security and protect their customers' sensitive financial information. Some of the examples are as below:

1. Many fintech apps use biometric authentication, such as facial recognition, fingerprint scanning, or voice recognition, to verify users' identities and provide an additional layer of security.

2. They are using advanced encryption techniques, such as end-to-end encryption, to protect data in transit and at rest. This ensures that even if a hacker gains access to the data, it will be unreadable.

3. Most of the Fintech companies are implementing 2FA, which requires users to provide a second form of verification, such as a code sent via SMS or an authenticator app, in addition to their password.
4. Some fintech companies are exploring the use of blockchain technology to secure transactions and protect sensitive information. Blockchain's decentralized and transparent nature makes it difficult for hackers to manipulate data.
5. Fintech companies are securing their APIs using techniques such as API keys, rate limiting, and input validation to prevent unauthorized access and data breaches.
6. Cloud security solutions, such as cloud-based firewalls and intrusion detection systems, are used to protect their data and applications in the cloud.
7. Fintech companies are using secure communication protocols, such as HTTPS and SSL/TLS, to encrypt data transmitted between their servers and users' devices.

Companies are continuously monitoring their systems for vulnerabilities and testing their security measures to ensure they're effective and up-to-date. By leveraging the new technologies, fintech companies can improve the security of their platforms, protect their customers' sensitive information, and maintain trust and confidence in their services.

Conclusion

In this chapter, we witnessed the history of banking and how it evolved from the nascent stages to a full-fledged Global industry driving world economies. We also looked at the different milestones during the evolution process. Globalization and the adaptation of Information Technology in Banking proved to be the main accelerators in this journey. The new technological advancements continue to bring in efficiencies and speed to enable further growth.

In the next Chapter, we will focus more on the technical aspects of Banking Solutions primarily around Cloud Computing. We will look at the advantages of hosting the solutions of cloud and discuss the different Service and Deployment models available on cloud.

Chapter 4
Introduction to Cloud Computing

In the earlier chapters, we have understood the types of financial services and how the banking industry has evolved over time. Now, let's shift our focus to look at how to implement IT solutions to support Banking Services.

Traditionally, IT solutions have been built and managed by the banks on their own IT infrastructure. Let's start with exploring cloud computing, why this is important, its characteristics and different models that can be leveraged.

In this chapter we will discuss the following aspects to get stared with our technical journey:

- Understanding Cloud Computing
- Characteristics of Cloud Computing
- Advantages of Cloud Computing
- Cloud Deployment Models
- Cloud Service Models
- Cloud Native Technologies

Understanding Cloud Computing

Cloud computing may be defined as services and resources that are offered by a Cloud Service Provider (such as storage, computer, infrastructure) that are available usually over the internet for use by customers.

Cloud computing has been fast evolving and maturing over the last couple of decades. Before we take a deep dive into the details of the cloud computing, lets understand what has led to its wide acceptance. Let's take an example of a startup bank, trying to build its IT systems in a traditional on-premise environment. First the architects need to analyze the requirements and estimate the amount of hardware and type of software required - for the short term and the long term scenarios. Once this is identified and approvals secured, they need to place orders for the hardware with the required specifications, and any software licenses. Depending on the vendor, this provisioning may take anywhere from few weeks to months.

Upon receiving the required hardware and software, the environment needs to be made ready (for hosting these servers). The engineering team and networking teams would be working together on setting up the required eco-system. This requires a significant upfront investment in the form of Capital Expenditure (Capex). Once setup, the organization will have to take care of all operations, security, upgrades, maintenance etc which requires latest technology know-how, and this increases the dependency on the people with those specialized skills.

Now, over the years, depending on how the bank is performing and the business is growing, the requirements would change, resulting in, let's say increased infrastructure requirements, which has to go through the same cycle of setting up. The infrastructure of the lower environments (like development and testing) might not be required the entire duration of the year, and may be sitting idle for significant periods of time.

Even in production, there may be periods of extended lull activities because of unforeseen situations like recession, pandemic, off-season etc. This would result in underutilized resources (that have already been procured and commissioned) during those periods. Also there can be periods of high spikes in activity, say during the shopping season, where the load on the resources is quite high. There may also be a requirement to restructure the resources due to enforcement of regulatory requirements like GDPR.

In a traditional setup, all these activities, require a lot of planning, estimation, predictions, investment, and technical know-how. With the current dynamic nature of the industry, the situation becomes more complex. The businesses would rather want to focus on implementing their business systems effectively rather than spending time, money and effort on setting up and managing the infrastructure to run those systems. Cloud Computing has evolved to address these issues, primarily by leveraging economies of scale, provision fit for purpose and based on established frameworks and best practices.

Brief history of Cloud Computing

The fundamental principles of cloud computing, such as resource pooling and economies of scale, have been around for decades. In the 1950s, when computing power and resources were scarce, expensive, and limited in size, not all organizations could afford to own and operate their own computing infrastructure. This led to the development of the concept of time-sharing, where multiple users could share the resources of a single machine, splitting the costs and benefits among them. This early form of cloud computing allowed companies to access powerful computing capabilities without having to invest in expensive hardware and maintenance.

Over the next two decades, the concept of shared resources evolved, transforming into a global network of computers that could share compute resources and data. The 1970s marked a significant milestone, as networked computing became more reliable and robust, giving rise to Virtual Machines. This innovation allowed multiple, logically separated computing environments to coexist on a single or few physical machines. The 1980s and 1990s were characterized by the dominance of Mainframe computers, with companies like International Business Machines (IBM) and Digital Equipment Corporation (DEC) offering remote computer services to businesses.

The late 1990s and early 2000s witnessed a surge in internet proliferation, and it was during this period that the term "Cloud Computing" is credited to have been coined by Professor Ramnath Chellappa. This era also saw the rise of Grid Computing, a concept that enabled the sharing of computing resources across multiple organizations. The widespread adoption of the internet and the emergence of shared resource usage laid the groundwork for the development of Cloud Computing as we know it today.

Modern Cloud Computing: The early 2000s marked a significant turning point in the evolution of Cloud Computing, with the launch of pioneering services that transformed the way applications were delivered over the internet. Salesforce. com, founded in 1999, was one of the first companies to offer Software as a Service (SaaS) application, while Amazon Web Services (AWS) launched in 2002, providing a web service platform for developers with a range of compute and storage services. This sparked a wave of innovation, as major technology companies like Google, IBM, Microsoft, and Oracle began offering cloud-based services. As a result, Cloud Computing became increasingly popular among individuals and organizations, who benefited from the flexibility, scalability, and cost-effectiveness of cloud-based solutions.

Since 2015, the landscape has continued to evolve, with the emergence of new technologies such as containers, microservices, artificial intelligence (AI), machine learning (ML), edge computing, and serverless computing. Today, Cloud Computing providers are offering specialized services and solutions that cater to these emerging technologies, further expanding the scope and capabilities of cloud-based computing.

Cloud Computing has reached a high level of maturity, with leading providers offering a vast array of services to customers. From the foundation of basic compute and storage capabilities to advanced services like pre-built AI and ML models, cloud providers have expanded their offerings to cater to a wide range of customer needs. As computing technology continues to evolve, Cloud Computing is also undergoing significant innovations, driven by breakthroughs in areas such as automation, artificial intelligence, machine learning, edge computing, and more. This ongoing evolution is enabling cloud providers to further enhance their services, delivering greater value to customers and pushing the boundaries of what is possible in the cloud.

In the next section, we will look at the characteristics of Cloud Computing, in comparison with the traditional approach

Characteristics of Cloud Computing

- Following are the typical characteristics of the Cloud Computing Services
    - **Pooling of Resources**: Cloud computing leverages the benefits of economies of scale by aggregating large quantities of resources, including hardware, proprietary software, and networking infrastructure. These resources are expertly managed by the service provider and dynamically allocated to multiple clients based on their individual demands and requirements. This enables the efficient and timely provisioning of services, ensuring a seamless and high-quality experience for users.
    - **Multi-Tenancy**: In a public cloud hosting environment, multiple tenants share the same resources. To ensure security and isolation, each tenant is separated from others, yet they can still access the necessary resources concurrently with other co-hosted tenants. Each tenant can utilize only the allocated resources, without affecting the performance of other tenants, thanks to the cloud's scalable and multi-tenant architecture.
    - **Virtualization**: The cloud's infrastructure is virtualized, allowing resources to be logically divided and isolated using specialized software and tools. This enables users to run multiple operating systems or different versions of the same software on the same physical resource, without being physically tied to a specific machine or environment.
    - On-Demand Self-Services: Cloud resources and services can be rapidly

provisioned, managed, and scaled on-demand through self-service interfaces. Users can interact with and manage these services through a variety of channels, including web-based portals, command-line interfaces (CLI), and application programming interfaces (API). This flexible approach enables users to access and control cloud resources in a convenient and efficient manner.

- Accessibility (Broad Network Access): Cloud resources can be accessed anywhere, anytime, from a wide range of devices that have an internet connection. This ability to provide secure and seamless access to cloud services from multiple devices and locations is known as Broad Network Access, enabling users to stay connected and productive from anywhere in the world. Most of the cloud service providers offer services in several regions spread across multiple continents. Users can choose one or a combination of several regions to run their workloads, depending on the business needs.

- Rapid Elasticity: Cloud resources offer unparalleled scalability, allowing them to be quickly scaled up or down as needed. This scaling can be automated, controlled manually, or scripted to ensure seamless and efficient resource allocation. Additionally, some cloud services, such as managed services and serverless computing, provide infinite scaling capabilities, enabling applications to adapt to changing demands without limitations.

- Measured Service: Cloud service providers offer advanced metering capabilities, enabling accurate measurement and tracking of resource usage. Customers can group usage metrics at various levels, from the entire tenant to individual applications. To ensure responsible usage, controls can be implemented to limit consumption of cloud resources and services. Additionally, intuitive dashboards are available, allowing users to monitor and manage their cloud services with ease.

- Pay-Per-Use Pricing: Cloud resources can be dynamically allocated and released as needed, allowing for flexible and efficient use of resources. With accurate usage tracking, users only pay for the resources they consume, ensuring cost-effectiveness. Cloud providers offer a variety of pricing models, catering to different services and usage scenarios, providing users with the flexibility to choose a pricing plan that best suits their needs. For instance, when using Virtual Machines, users can choose the amount of compute power, the memory and associated storage. Based on the chosen configuration, the users are changed by a unit of time, as defined by the Cloud Provider. Once the resources is no longer required, the user can shut down the instances and remove the associated storage. This will ensure that no charges are being levied when the services are not in use.

- Security: Cloud providers implement robust security measures, comprising multiple layers of defense-in-depth. This ensures that cloud-based resources and services are protected from various threats and vulnerabilities. This comprehensive approach includes physical security, firewalls, network and data encryption, application security, tenant isolation, vulnerability scanning, digital certificates, secrets management, and regular updates and patch management.

- Resiliency and Availability: Cloud Service Providers offer a range of techniques and features that enable clients to ensure high availability and resiliency in their applications. By leveraging strategies such as distributing workload across regions, data backups, load balancing, and more, applications can quickly recover from disruptions, ensuring minimal downtime and maximum uptime.

The above features are powerful tools for building robust, secure, scalable, cost-efficient solutions on cloud. But to make best use of them and to be able to build an effective system, it requires a thorough understanding of the cloud offerings and the associated design patterns. We will look at the design considerations in the later chapters of this book.

Advantages of Cloud Computing

Now that we have seen what Cloud Computing is about and its characteristics, let's look at why it is relevant by understanding its advantages.

- Cost Effective and simple: Establishing new infrastructure on-premise can be a costly and intricate process, requiring substantial upfront capital expenditures (capex) and specialized technical expertise for installation and configuration. Moreover, the procured hardware often becomes obsolete, making it challenging to dispose of it when no longer needed. Additionally, on-premise infrastructure requires significant real-estate costs, as well as expenses for electricity, cooling, physical security, and other services. In contrast, cloud offerings provide a more cost-effective and efficient solution, allowing for quick and easy setup compared to building a dedicated data center on-premises. With cloud services, there is no need to wait for processes like order creation, availability, and shipping, thereby reducing the overall time and cost of implementation. For example, as per the report from AWS, Enterprise Strategy Group validated that organizations reduced computer, networking, and storage costs by up to 66% by migrating from on premises to AWS Cloud Infrastructure. Link to the report: https:// d1.awsstatic.com/AWS%20Cloud%20Storage/ESG-Economic-Validation- -Maximizing-Economic-Advantages-by-Migrating-to-AWS-Cloud- Infrastructure.pdf
- Pay-per-use: Cloud services operate on a pay-per-use model, where you only pay for the resources, you utilize. This eliminates the drawbacks of underutilized resources, which can sit idle and unused. To ensure cost

control, budgeting alerts can be set up to monitor and limit resource usage and service consumption. This flexible pricing approach makes it an effective way to manage costs in scenarios where budget constraints are a concern. For example, Google's Speech-to-Text v2 API, Standard recognition model costs about $0.016 / 1 minute, per 1 month / account. Users need to pay only for their usage of the service.

- Rapid elasticity: In traditional on-premises environments, it's necessary to plan and provision resources well in advance. However, this approach can lead to difficulties in achieving elasticity, as it often requires procuring additional resources, which can be a challenge, especially for short-term or temporary needs. For instance, when a sudden surge in demand occurs, such as during a holiday season or a specific project phase (like temporary Test environment) , it can be difficult to quickly scale up resources. In contrast, cloud resources offer highly scalable and flexible capabilities, allowing them to scale up or down in real-time to match changing demands. This means that resources can be dynamically allocated or deallocated as needed, eliminating the need for lengthy planning and provisioning cycles.

- High Availability: Cloud providers guarantee high availability, as stated in their Service Level Agreements (SLAs). They achieve this by leveraging massive resource pooling, which is a complex and challenging feat to replicate in a single-tenant on-premises environment. For example, IBM Cloud Event Streams service is provided with an availability SLA of 99.99% on the Standard Plan.

- Range of services: Cloud providers offer a diverse range of services, encompassing compute, networking, software, middleware, operations (such as monitoring and logging), security, and automation. This comprehensive suite of services enables you to select the precise resources and capabilities that best meet your unique needs and requirements, simplifying the process of building and maintaining your applications and infrastructure. For example, from data warehousing to deployment tools, directories to content delivery, there are over 200 services offered for user consumption on AWS platform.

- Global reach: Imagine a European bank expanding its services to South America, requiring the setup of new infrastructure in a distant geography. Establishing physical resources in a new location can be a daunting and complex task. In contrast, cloud services offer a virtual and globally accessible infrastructure that can be easily set up and replicated across different regions. Resources can be easily setup at any geography as offered by the Cloud Provider, and a setup from an existing system can be quicky replicated to the new environment, saving time, cost and providing reliability. For example, Azure has more than 60 announced regions globally for use by customers.

The numerous benefits of cloud computing have contributed to its widespread adoption over the past few decades. We have explored the "what" and "why" of cloud computing. Now, let's dive into the "how" by examining the various cloud computing models available, in the next sections of this chapter.

Cloud Deployment Models

Depending on where the cloud applications are deployed, how they are managed and with whom they are shared with, there are the following Cloud Deployment Models.

Public Cloud

This is the most common form of deployment model where the resources are hosted on the datacenters owned by a third-party cloud provider. Registered customers can subscribe to the offered resources and services and they are virtually accessible over the public internet.

This is an optimal form of resource pooling, where the resources are distributed among various datacenters that are spread across the globe. Since the resources are owned and managed by the Cloud Provider on a massive scale, they are most optimized and result in lesser cost, better performance (like scaling and throughput) and (almost) infinite capacity. The services are shared by multiple customers and are accessible by a pay-per-use model.

Public cloud solutions may be suitable for businesses and applications which do not have stringent compliance requirements. Some potential Enterprise Use-cases:

- Web Hosting and Application Deployment
- Hosting Lower environments (Development and Testing)
- Data Storage and Backup
- Disaster Recovery and Business Continuity
- Large data processing like IOT
- Process intensive workloads (AI/ML, Big Data Analytics).

Private Cloud

This model offers dedicated cloud resources to individual customers. The resources are assigned exclusively for a single customer and helps them meet any regulatory compliance requirements to isolate their workloads from external parties.

Privatization of cloud services can be achieved in the following ways:

- Virtual Private Cloud (VPC): Here the resources are physically hosted on the shared Public Cloud, but the customer can group a set of their cloud resources into an isolated network. Components in a VPC may be globally distributed, but can still communicate with each other using internal network addresses (IPs), without the need for traffic to traverse public internet. Traffic flowing in and out of the network is controlled by using Firewalls and can be monitored via logs. So, even though the resources are co hosted with others, they are privately accessible to a single customer. This allows to take advantage of the resource pooling offered by the public cloud, but still privately access and control them.
- Physical Private Cloud: Here the resources are physically isolated and are purely dedicated to a single organization. This can either be:
  - on-premise private cloud, where the resources are hosted on customers' on-premise infrastructure. This offers the highest level of security and isolation for the organization and are fully under their control. But the cloud features are limited by the capacity of the customer's available infrastructure and may impact the performance. This is different than traditional on-premise infrastructure in a way that in a private cloud environment, the resources are better optimized and efficiently managed using the tools and services provided by the cloud provider (like monitoring, IAM (Identity and Access Management), resource optimization and resource allocation, etc.)
  - off-premise, where the resources are hosted at the cloud provider's data centers on a hardware setup that is dedicated for a customer. This setup is owned and managed by the cloud provider and so, offers better cost and resource optimization.

Some potential Enterprise Use-cases:

- Processing and hosting of Secure and confidential data
- Regulatory Compliance and Data Sovereignty
- Intranet Applications
- Highly customizable infrastructure requirements
- Integration with Legacy Systems
- Research and Development.

Hybrid Cloud

Not all applications of an organization are suitable to be hosted on Public Cloud. For various business reasons, there can be scenarios where organizations are required to host some of their applications on Private Cloud, but would still want to leverage the benefits of Public Cloud for other suitable applications. A Hybrid Cloud is a cloud computing environment where applications run on more than one set of distributed computing resources. This is usually a combination of on-premises, private and public cloud solutions integrated seamlessly into single environment. This topic will be discussed further in detail in the chapter 'Designing Banking Cloud solutions.'.

Multi Cloud

A Multi Cloud model is one which uses a combination of services from multiple Public Cloud vendors like Google, AWS, Azure, etc. This pattern is suitable when you want to reduce the dependency on a single cloud provider, help avoid vendor lock-in and increase the flexibility of choosing the appropriate services. This option also provides flexibility to leverage the best features of different cloud providers depending on the requirements.

The distributed models like Hybrid and Multi Cloud get very complex to design, implement and manage as the requests / data for a single transaction may traverse through more than one network and geography, resulting in security and latency challenges. We will look at the best practices later in this book when we discuss solution designing.

Some potential Enterprise Use-cases for Hybrid Cloud and Multi Cloud implementations:

- Reduce dependency on single provider / single hosting environment
- Data backups
- High Availability / Disaster Recovery
- Separation of Hosting of Process intensive workloads from Data.

Community Cloud

Organizations belonging to a sector (like Banking, Healthcare, Education) have specialized needs to managing their IT systems and they may sometimes require sharing of common data among other peers.

Community Cloud Model offers a solution for this, by providing a hosting environment, resources, and services that are tailor-made for organizations with similar compliance, regulatory and operational requirements.

Following are examples of pre-defined Community Cloud offerings.:

- AWS GovCloud (US)
- Azure Government Top Secret
- Health Cloud by Salesforce
- IBM Watson Health

- IBM Financial Services Cloud
- Google for Education

Community cloud models are more cost effective than Private cloud because of the resource sharing. The cloud services may be provided and managed by a third-party provider on behalf of the community or could be self-managed by the tenants of the community. Governance plays a critical role in this model for setting up, managing and ensuring compliance of the Governance Policies.

Cloud Service Models

Cloud providers offer three primary cloud service models, also known as cloud service offerings, to enable organizations to outsource infrastructure, platform, and software responsibilities. These models cater to diverse customer needs, allowing them to subscribe to the services that best suit their requirements and pay only for the resources and services consumed.

While offloading infrastructure, platform, and software responsibilities to a cloud provider offers numerous benefits, there are also limitations. Since these components are owned and managed by the cloud provider, customers may have limited or no control over certain aspects, such as the physical location, maintenance schedule, operating system or middleware versions, and patch management.

Infrastructure As A Service (IaaS)

This is the foundational layer of cloud computing, where the cloud provider offers on-demand access to the underlying infrastructure, including networking, servers, compute resources, storage, and memory. The cloud provider is responsible for hosting and managing these components in their data centers, which can be located across multiple geographic locations.

Customers can select from a range of options, including computing power, memory, storage, networking speed, and hosting location. These resources are virtually accessible over the internet, providing flexibility and scalability. However, customers are limited by the options and restrictions imposed by the cloud provider, which may not offer complete control over the infrastructure. Nevertheless, customers still have control over the platform and software layers, allowing them to customize and manage their applications as needed.

This model is well-suited for scenarios where raw infrastructure is required, such as:

- High data storage needs, such as backups.

- Running process-intensive workloads, like machine learning.
- Custom services that require control over the platform and software

In these cases, IaaS provides the necessary flexibility and control over the underlying infrastructure, allowing customers to tailor their infrastructure to meet specific needs.

In the infrastructure-as-a-service (IaaS) model, cloud providers offer virtualized computing resources, including virtual servers, memory, storage and networking. Some examples of IaaS offerings from leading cloud providers include:

- Virtual Machines: Amazon EC2 (Elastic Compute Cloud), Azure Virtual Machines, Google Compute Engine, and IBM Virtual Servers.
- Storage: Amazon S3 (Simple Storage Service), Azure Blob Storage, Google Cloud Storage, and IBM Cloud Object Storage.
- Networking: Amazon VPC, Google Cloud VPC, Azure Virtual Network, IBM Cloud VPC

Platform As A Service (PaaS)

This is the next level of abstraction, built on top of IaaS. In PaaS, the cloud provider offers a complete platform for building and running applications, including the operating system, software, application servers, middleware, and application runtimes. This means that developers can focus on writing code without worrying about the underlying infrastructure, as the platform is fully managed by the cloud provider.

From the provided options, customers can choose which OS to run on, which Database to use, which Application Server to host the services on and which Programming Language runtime to use. These options can be easily provisioned and configured through self-service portals provided by the cloud service provider. However, customers are limited by the versions of the services offered, with older versions being decommissioned once newer versions become available. This means that customers must keep their applications updated and compatible with the latest offered versions, as the cloud provider may not maintain older versions.

This model is ideal for customers who need to quickly develop and deploy end-to-end applications. With PaaS, application teams can focus on writing code and implementing business logic, rather than spending time on setting up the environment. This allows them to be more productive and efficient, and to deliver applications faster and more reliably.

Some Popular PaaS Offering:

- Google Cloud App Engine, Cloud Run,
- AWS Elastic Beanstalk, Amazon RDS

- Azure App Service, Azure Logic Apps
- IBM Cloud AIPaaS (PaaS for Artificial Intelligence), iPaaS (integration platform as a service), cPaaS (communications platform as a service), mPaaS (mobile platform as a service)

Software as a Service (SaaS)

This is the topmost layer of abstraction, built on top of the PaaS Platform. Here, the software is provided as a service, where the service provider manages and runs the entire product, end-to-end. This means that customers can access and use the software without having to install, configure, or maintain it themselves. Examples of SaaS offerings include:

- Shopify, which allows customers to build ecommerce websites without writing code or managing systems.
- Salesforce and HubSpot, which offer customer relationship management software.
- Gmail, which provides email services.
- Zoom and Webex, which offer video conferencing platforms

In each of these cases, the SaaS provider offers a user-friendly interface for customizing the application, allowing customers to focus on their specific needs and goals without worrying about the underlying technology.

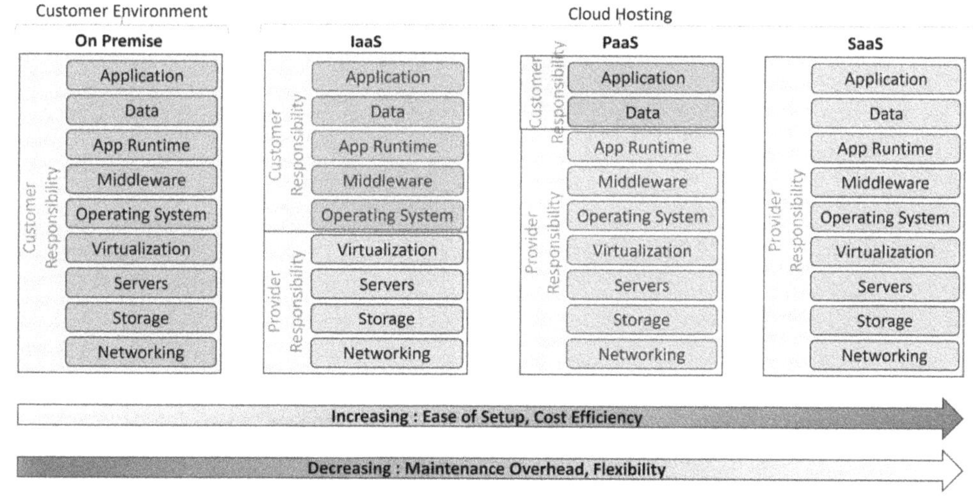

Figure 4.1: Comparison of features across Cloud Service Models

The Software as a Service (SaaS) model offers a convenient and easy way to run a system using pre-configured and ready-to-use software. However, customers are limited in their flexibility and customization options, as they are constrained by the features and options available in the provided software.

Some Popular SaaS offerings:

- AWS CyberArk (Identity Security Platform)
- Google Workspace
- Slack (for messaging)
- Dropbox (for file storage and sharing)

To understand the Cloud Service Models a bit more, let's consider a simple and common non-banking use case: "Setting up an E-commerce website" and walkthrough the different scenarios.

So what does it take to build an ecommerce website from scratch?

Infrastructure: Procure and configure Servers, Networking, Storage, Compute power, Virtualization. This includes maintenance and operations like electricity, backups and security.

Platform: Once the Infrastructure is in place, we need to setup the platform required to build and run the system. This includes Operating system, Middleware (like databases, application servers, message-queues) and Runtime (e.g. Java JRE).

Software: After the Platform is setup, next is to design, build, run and operate the system which includes the application and data. This includes setting up data and application security (like access management, virus scans, encryption, etc).

Each layer above is built on top of its preceding layer. Once the system is built and ready there would be maintenance and operations required at each layer, like adding more memory or compute, patch management of the software, version upgrades, introducing functional changes and enhancements. In a traditional on-premises setup, you need to manage all the three layers. But, by leveraging an appropriate Cloud Service Model, Organizations can offload few or all of these responsibilities to the cloud provider.

Now that we have understood the basics of cloud computing, in the next section, we will see how to make the best use of these resources and services.

Cloud Native Technologies

So far, we've discussed Cloud offerings as a set of virtual resources and services available over the internet. This suggests that customers can run any system on this platform. Then what does be 'Cloud Native' mean?

While Cloud can support a wide range of workloads, applications built using traditional or legacy technologies may not be well-suited for the Cloud. In fact, they may not fully leverage the Cloud's benefits or may even experience performance issues due to the Cloud's inherently less controlled environment.

Legacy applications, built using traditional development methodologies, often exhibit monolithic architectures, characterized by:.

- Long build, test, and deploy cycles.
- Tight coupling with other components, leading to complex interdependencies.
- Cumbersome development processes, resulting in inefficient systems and slower time-to-market.

These traditional approaches have led to the creation of inflexible, rigid systems that are challenging to maintain, update, and scale. The rigid architecture and complex dependencies make it difficult to introduce changes or improvements, which can result in longer development cycles and slower go-to-market times. This can hinder an organization's ability to respond quickly to changing market demands and customer needs. To truly harness the power of the Cloud, applications must be designed with Cloud Native principles in mind.

Cloud Native Applications are those, that are build using a set of architectural practices and programming models that help to leverage the full potential of Cloud, like building smaller services, that are container based, loosely coupled, independently scalable, testable and support quick deployments. This helps in building more efficient, highly available, rapidly scalable, robust, quickly deployable, portable systems, to effectively support the fast-changing business needs.

Below are few of the Cloud Native Technologies that have gained wide acceptance

- Containers and Orchestration: Containers are self-contained, lightweight packages of software that ensure consistency and reliability across various environments. By packaging the software and its dependencies, including the operating system, containers guarantee that the package will execute consistently across different environments. Docker is a prominent container platform that has gained widespread adoption.
- Container orchestration platforms, such as open-source Kubernetes, take container management to the next level by automating tasks like deployment, scaling, and operations. These platforms provide a centralized way to manage and coordinate the deployment of multiple containers, ensuring seamless

and efficient management of containerized applications.
- Microservices: This is an architectural style that involves breaking down an application into smaller, independent services that can be developed, deployed, and scaled independently. Each service is designed to serve a specific business purpose and can interact with other services through APIs.

This approach offers several benefits, including:

- Polyglot programming, where different services can be developed using the most suitable technologies
- Independent scalability, allowing different functions to scale according to their unique requirements
- Fault isolation, where a failure in one service does not necessarily impact the entire system
- Faster go-to-market, as each granular service can be owned and deployed by a self-sufficient team
- Enhanced security, as not all functions are exposed to external users

However, Microservices design is very complex, and the implementation presents its own set of challenges, such as:

- Managing interservice communication.
- Added latency due to multiple service invocations
- Load balancing between several service instances
- Internal security and access control
- Service registry and discovery

To address these challenges, a ServiceMesh layer like Istio can be introduced, providing a unified platform for managing and orchestrating Microservices.

- Devops: Automating the continuous integration and continuous delivery (CI/CD) pipeline enables faster, more reliable, and predictable software delivery, covering all phases of the software development life cycle (SDLC) from development to production. This process involves integrating multiple tools and technologies, including:
    o Version control systems like GitHub for managing code repositories.
    o Build tools like Jenkins for automating the build process.
    o Infrastructure as Code (IaC) tools like Terraform for managing infrastructure provisioning.
    o CI/CD tools like CircleCI for automating testing, deployment, and delivery

By automating the CI/CD pipeline, organizations can streamline software delivery, reduce manual errors, and increase collaboration among development teams. This enables faster time-to-market, improved quality, and enhanced customer satisfaction.

- API Management: Services are typically exposed as APIs via REST (Representational State Transfer) services, which provide a standardized way of interacting with the service. These services are typically stateless, meaning that each request contains all the information necessary to complete the request, and they serve to realize a specific business function, such as creating a new user in the system.
  To manage and secure these APIs, gateways like Kong are used. These gateways provide a range of features, including:
  - Rate limiting: controlling the number of requests that can be made to an API within a certain time period.
  - Authentication:
  - Monitoring and Analytics: Monitoring API performance and availability providing insights into API usage and performance.
  - Logs: logging API requests and responses for auditing and troubleshooting purposes.
  - Security: Providing encryption, SSL/TLS termination, and other security features like verifying the identity of requests and ensuring that only authorized requests are processed
  - Versioning and Path-based routing: Routing requests to specific services or versions of services based on the path of the request
- Serverless Computing: This is also known as Function as a Service, is a cloud computing model that enables developers to run small, independent pieces of code without the need to provision or manage any underlying infrastructure. This means that developers can focus solely on writing the code, without worrying about the infrastructure required to run it. Serverless computing platforms, such as AWS Lambda, Azure Functions, and Google Cloud Functions, offer a range of benefits, including:
  - Infinite scalability: Serverless computing platforms can automatically scale to handle changes in workload, ensuring that your code can handle large volumes of traffic.
  - Cost-effective: You only pay for the compute time consumed by your code, rather than provisioning and maintaining servers.
  - Simplified development: Developers can focus on writing code, without worrying about the underlying infrastructure.
- Extended Storage options: The cloud offers a range of unconventional storage solutions that cater to diverse needs. One such solution is object storage, which allows users to store any type of file, regardless of its size or format. Object storage solutions like AWS S3 and Google Cloud Storage are particularly cost-effective and scalable, making them ideal for large-scale data storage needs.

Another innovative storage solution is distributed databases, which offer unprecedented scalability and virtually unlimited capacity. Distributed databases like Google Cloud Spanner enable users to store and process massive amounts of data, while providing high availability and reliability. These databases are designed to handle complex queries and provide real-time insights, making them an attractive option for businesses that require robust data analytics capabilities.

- Edge Computing: Edge Computing is a distributed computing model that enables data processing closer to its source, reducing latency and improving application performance. This approach is particularly beneficial for applications that require real-time processing, such as IoT devices, and those that demand low latency, such as caching. Additionally, edge computing is well-suited for applications that require high bandwidth, such as processing static data.
- Observability and Monitoring: In today's automated systems, monitoring and observing services and infrastructure is crucial for swift issue resolution and efficient operations. To achieve this, automated systems continuously scan system logs to detect any anomalies or issues and display them on a dashboard for easy visualization. Once an issue is identified, automated corrective actions can be taken, or notifications can be sent to the operations team. This enables rapid response and minimizes downtime. Some popular tools used for monitoring and alerting include Prometheus, which provides monitoring and alerting capabilities, and Grafana, which offers visualization and dashboarding capabilities to support Prometheus. Jaeger, a distributed tracing tool, is also used to monitor and debug complex systems.

Cloud Native Computing Foundation (CNCF) is an open sources project started in 2015 to help organizations advance in their cloud-native technology adoption. Its founding members include Google, IBM, RedHat, Intel and other prominent technology companies.

The details of the 'Graduated Projects' under CNCF can be found at https://www.cncf.io/projects/ . We can see from the list that the focus is not just on using a particular programming language or a set of defined services, but it heavily promotes the use of containers and related technologies, including interface components for exposing services via APIs, DevOps, Microservices, Interservice communication, Serverless functions, Monitoring and Self-healing systems.

Conclusion

In this chapter, you have been introduced with the basic concepts of cloud computing. We have discussed what cloud computing is about, its importance, different models available to choose from and how to implement solutions using cloud native technologies. With this foundation, we will move on to more advanced concepts like understanding the challenges faced in the cloud journey, designing effective cloud solutions and the associated best practices, in the subsequent chapters of this book.

References

https://www.geeksforgeeks.org/characteristics-of-cloud-computing/
https://herovired.com/learning-hub/blogs/characteristics-of-cloud-computing/
https://unstop.com/blog/characteristics-of-cloud-computing
https://www.javatpoint.com/features-of-cloud-computing
https://www.techtarget.com/searchcloudcomputing/feature/7-key-characteristics-of-cloud-computing
https://www.spiceworks.com/tech/cloud/articles/what-is-community-cloud/
https://cloud.google.com/discover/what-is-a-private-cloud
https://aws.amazon.com/what-is/cloud-native/
https://medium.com/threat-intel/cloud-computing-e5e746b282f5
https://en.wikipedia.org/wiki/Cloud_computing

Chapter 5
Challenges of moving Banking workloads to Cloud

In the previous chapter, we have understood the basics of cloud computing and the associated advantages. While cloud computing presents numerous benefits, it is not a one-size-fits-all solution. Banks may still encounter challenges as they embark on their cloud adoption journey.

Before we delve into the design of cloud-based IT solutions, it is essential to acknowledge and understand the common hurdles that banks may face when migrating their workloads to the cloud. This will enable organizations to better prepare for and address these challenges, ultimately ensuring a smoother and more successful cloud adoption experience.

In this chapter we will discuss the following aspects to understand what potential hindrances in the cloud journey could be:

- Key drivers for banks to try adopting cloud computing
- Typical challenges in implementing IT solutions
- Why Cloud Adaptation Fails?
- Guiding Principles and Frameworks

Key drivers for banks to try adopting cloud computing.

In the previous chapter, we explored the benefits of cloud computing. Now, let's delve into the reasons why banks are increasingly turning to cloud migration for their IT solutions. What drives this trend, what are the key motivators behind this shift and the imminent need for banks to upgrade the traditional services and associated IT Systems.

- **Evolving Customer Expectations**: In today's digitally savvy era, customers have unprecedented access to information, empowering them to make more informed financial decisions. The current generation of customers is tech-savvy and expects seamless, convenient, and personalized banking experiences. Gone are the days of tedious physical forms and lengthy processes for loan applications, account openings, or performing financial transactions. Instead, customers now increasingly demand self-service options, pre-filled information on their devices, and tailored experiences tailored to their unique financial profiles, including spending habits, goals, income sources, and more.

- **Increasing Competition and difficulty in retaining customers**: In today's competitive market, customers have a plethora of options to choose from, driven by factors such as brand reputation, stability, transparency, customer service, and more. As customers' expectations continue to rise, Financial Institutions face significant challenges in maintaining customer loyalty and staying ahead of the competition. To attract new customers and retain existing ones, they must consistently deliver exceptional experiences. Furthermore, the widespread adoption of social media has created a powerful platform for customers to share their experiences, both positive and negative, with a vast audience. This can have a profound impact on a Financial Institution's reputation, making it crucial for them to prioritize customer satisfaction and loyalty to avoid negative word-of-mouth and maintain a competitive edge.

- **Competition from non-traditional sectors**: Financial transactions are progressively shifting away from traditional paper-based methods, with electronic transactions becoming the norm. Non-traditional financial institutions, such as mobile network providers, now offer innovative payment solutions, eliminating the need for physical bank branches. Digital innovation has significantly impacted the banking industry, disrupting traditional practices and intensifying competition.

- **Technological changes:** To address the evolving technological landscape and solve traditional challenges, legacy applications must be updated and modernized. By implementing modern solutions, such as automation, self-service systems (like kiosks and mobile apps), artificial intelligence, machine learning, and fraud detection tools, financial institutions can provide personalized services and create better customer experiences. Delaying adaptation to these advancements poses a significant risk, as outdated systems may struggle to meet the demands of modern customers and competitors.

- **Regulations**: As financial processes evolve and technology adoption increases, the associated risks also grow in number and complexity. Regulatory bodies are responding by implementing stricter policies and regulations to address these concerns. Financial institutions are therefore required to comply with a diverse array of regulatory and compliance requirements, such as data collection and storage limitations, secure storage and disclosure guidelines, Know Your Customer (KYC) procedures, and more. Meeting these demands often involves intricate and challenging implementation efforts.

- **Cybersecurity**: Cybercriminals are continuously devising new methods to perpetrate financial crimes, leading to compromised data, damaged reputations, and substantial financial losses for both financial institutions and their customers. These fraudulent activities can be caused by both internal and external cyber threats. To effectively address these cybersecurity risks and implement proactive safeguarding measures, financial institutions should strengthen their processes and incorporate cutting-edge technology to enhance the security of financial transactions.

These are compelling reasons for banks to modernize their traditional IT infrastructure, with cloud computing emerging as a potential solution. As we discussed earlier, cloud computing offers a range of services and design options that can help banks overcome these issues, making it an attractive option for those seeking to upgrade their IT capabilities and stay competitive in today's digital landscape.

Typical challenges in upgrading IT Solutions

Transitioning to upgraded IT solutions can be met with resistance, and financial institutions often encounter various challenges throughout this process. Technical difficulties, cultural barriers, and process-oriented obstacles are common hurdles. In this chapter, we will focus on the challenges related to IT solutions upgrades. These challenges may include data migration issues, integrating new systems with existing infrastructure, and ensuring user adoption and training. Overcoming these challenges requires careful planning, execution, and a well-thought-out strategy. The focus here would be on IT solutions and does not cover the more generic challenges and risks faced by Financial Institutions like, laws, Non-Performing Assets, NPA, Bad loans, scams, etc.

Financial institutions must swiftly adjust to the changing landscape due to intensifying competition and rising customer expectations. To achieve this, they must foster a cultural shift across their organization that encourages understanding, appreciation, and adaptation to rapid changes in areas such as customer service, service offerings, and technological adaptation. This includes embracing omnichannel services to cater to diverse customer needs and preferences.

Transitioning financial solutions to the cloud can necessitate substantial alterations to business processes and workflows, posing considerable challenges for financial institutions. These changes may involve updating existing systems, integrating new cloud-based tools into the ecosystem, and altering employee responsibilities. Effective project management, clear communication, and a well-defined transition plan are crucial to ensuring a smooth and successful migration.

Ensuring the security and integrity of applications and data on cloud-based financial solutions is a major technical challenge for banks. Financial institutions are subject to stringent regulations and security requirements, which add to the complexity of securing cloud-based environments. Financial data is sensitive and regulated, and organizations may be concerned about storing and processing it in a cloud environment that is outside of their direct control. Robust security strategies need to be implemented for overcoming these Security, Data Sovereignty and Compliance challenges.

The overall migration strategy should be viewed as a long-term investment rather than a short-term and ad hoc solution. Proper planning, budgeting, and ongoing cost management are essential to maximizing the return on investment and ensuring long-term success.

Implementing cloud-based financial solutions may necessitate a distinct cost structure and budgeting methodology, which can be challenging for organizations accustomed to traditional on-premises systems. Cloud migrations may require a more flexible budgeting approach, as costs can be more unpredictable and variable than with traditional on-premises solutions, unless properly planned for.

Although cloud solutions can offer significant cost savings through reduced capital expenditures, there are often hidden costs associated with their implementation. These can include:

- Training: Employees may require training to effectively use and manage cloud-based tools and applications.

- Upgrades: Keeping cloud-based systems up-to-date with the latest features and security patches can require additional investment.
- Migration: Transitioning from on-premises systems to the cloud can involve significant migration costs, including the cost of rewriting applications to work in a cloud environment.
- Ongoing Costs: Cloud-based solutions often come with additional operational costs, such as data transfer fees, usage charges, and support and maintenance agreements.

These hidden costs should be thoroughly evaluated and incorporated into the comprehensive financial assessment of cloud migration projects. Effective controls must be established to prevent cost overruns resulting from mismanagement of resource utilization. This can be accomplished through:

- Resource Allocation: Efficient allocation of resources based on workload and demand can help prevent overutilization and underutilization.
- Monitoring and Reporting: Regular monitoring and reporting of resource utilization can help identify trends and anomalies, allowing for corrective action to be taken promptly.
- Optimization: Regular optimization of resource usage can help reduce waste and improve efficiency.

In a Hybrid cloud model, banks might prefer to maintain their core-banking systems on-premises. This requires exposing specific features such as easily consumable and extendable services and establishing complex integrations between the cloud and on-premises systems. This also introduces networking, integration and security challenges.

To successfully navigate their cloud adoption journey, organizations should anticipate and proactively address these potential challenges by developing a comprehensive and robust IT solution migration strategy, ensuring a seamless transition and minimizing the risk of setbacks.

While meticulous planning and due diligence are essential for a successful cloud adoption journey, leaders must also acknowledge that setbacks and failures can still occur. To mitigate these risks, leaders should cultivate a mindset that anticipates and prepares for challenging situations, integrating this perspective into their overall strategy. When unforeseen obstacles arise, teams should engage in a reflective process, seek expert guidance, and leverage best practices to identify and rectify issues. This may require adjusting course, resetting goals, and making necessary changes to stay on track, ultimately ensuring a successful cloud implementation and minimizing the risk of prolonged delays or failures.

Why Cloud Adaptation Fails?

Each organization may have their own short term and long-term goals to achieve the cloud migration of their IT solutions. For some applications, hosting a static website on cloud could be the goal, while for other, streaming of real time IOT data and running complex analysis on it could be the goal. The success of a cloud migration can be measured by its ability to meet established goals, such as improved efficiency, enhanced agility, or better cost management, depending on the specific objectives of the organization. Many enterprises, particularly those new to cloud adoption, face challenges in achieving their desired outcomes and frequently fail to meet their objectives. There can be multiple reasons that could result in failed cloud-adoption exercise, that we will discuss below.

- Lack of Vision: Implementing a successful cloud strategy requires a clear vision and well-defined goals. Organizations should articulate a clear vision of their current state, short-term and long-term goals, and a structured roadmap to achieve them. Adopting a new technology, like cloud computing, requires careful consideration and planning. A haphazard approach, driven by trends alone, is unlikely to yield optimal results. Leaders should steer clear of following cloud trends without proper evaluation to ensure the best possible outcomes for the organization.
- Internal communication: Once a cloud strategy is established, it is essential to communicate it clearly across the organization. For organizations in the early stages of their cloud maturity, this may involve a significant cultural shift. Ensuring that employees understand and adapt to this change is crucial for a successful cloud journey.
- Ineffective Governance: Project Governance acts as a compass, guiding the decision-making process and ensuring clear accountability and responsibility assignments for the Cloud Adaptation project. Effective Project Governance is a crucial framework that outlines the decision-making process, clarifies roles, and assigns responsibilities to ensure accountability. This helps in ensuring timely decision-making, and keeps stakeholders aligned, ultimately driving project success. Without a well-established governance structure, the Cloud Adaptation process can quickly become disjointed, leading to missed targets and potential project failures.
- Improper design of cloud solutions: It's a common misconception that cloud services are inherently cheap and simple to implement due to the abundance of self-service choices and options available. However, the success of a cloud adaptation depends on its thoughtful design and implementation. It's essential to carefully select services that align with desired outcomes and to prioritize key non-functional aspects such as security, performance, and scalability from the outset. Additionally, thorough testing is crucial to ensure

the solution meets both known (based on requirements) and unknown (based on best practices) scenarios, ultimately delivering a reliable and effective cloud solution.

- Challenges associated with Data Migrations: Cloud migration is often necessary in various situations, including migrating data for existing applications, storing data backups, and setting up data replication for high availability. These tasks typically involve complex processes that demand careful planning to ensure efficient management of costs, data integrity, and performance. When transferring live or incremental data, data integrity is paramount, and when taking live backups or performing live data migrations, performance optimization is critical. Proper planning and execution are essential to minimize disruptions, maintain data accuracy, and achieve optimal results in cloud migration scenarios.

- Challenges associated with Application Migrations: Many financial institutions rely on legacy core banking systems that have been in place for decades, often accompanied by challenges such as incomplete or outdated application documentation, and high dependence on a few key individuals who manage the systems. When attempting to migrate these applications to the cloud, additional hurdles arise, including the need for refactoring and addressing interoperability issues. Moreover, the lack of a comprehensive migration strategy can be a significant obstacle to successful cloud adoption, leading to increased risk of project failure. To overcome these challenges, it's essential to develop a well-planned and executed cloud migration strategy that considers the unique complexities of legacy systems.

- Being skeptical about cloud journey: Despite the benefits of cloud computing, many organizations still rely heavily on business-critical systems running on non-cloud environments. This is often due to misconceptions about the capabilities and offerings of Cloud Service Providers, leading to the development of partial and inefficient suboptimal systems that are only partially migrated to the cloud. As a result, organizations may be missing out on the scalability, flexibility, and cost savings that cloud computing can provide, and may be facing unnecessary complexity and risk because of their limited cloud adoption.

- Single Cloud Strategy: Some organizations may be overly reliant on a single Cloud Service Provider, failing to take full advantage of hybrid cloud and multi-cloud strategies. Each cloud provider has its unique strengths and offerings, and a thorough analysis is necessary to select the best features and services for a particular organization's needs. By not properly evaluating and leveraging multiple cloud providers, organizations may be limiting their flexibility, scalability, and innovation, as well as exposing themselves to potential vendor lock-in and single-point-of-failure risks. A well-planned hybrid and multi-cloud approach can help organizations optimize their cloud strategy, balance risks, optimize cost and ensure greater agility and

resilience.
- Skill gaps: Adapting to cloud computing requires a distinct set of technological skills that differ from those needed for traditional legacy implementations. Not only do cloud-native technologies need to be implemented, but significant automation is also necessary to streamline implementation, testing, and deployment. To achieve the best outcomes, it's essential to leverage available cloud services and assets effectively and this requires proficiency in designing effective cloud solutions. To support this, employees must be trained and up skilled to work with new technologies and processes. This training should be an ongoing process throughout the cloud adoption lifecycle, ensuring that skills remain current and aligned with evolving cloud technologies and best practices.

In the next few chapters of this book, we will look at best practices and design principles to avoid such failures.

Guiding Principles and Frameworks

To help organizations overcome their cloud adaptation challenges, the major Cloud Providers provide guiding architectural principles and reusable frameworks to guide the tenants on their cloud adoption. Below are few examples

- AWS Well Architected Tools: https://aws.amazon.com/well-architected-tool/
- Google Cloud Architecture Framework: https://cloud.google.com/architecture/framework
- Azure Well-Architected Framework: https://learn.microsoft.com/en-us/azure/well-architected/

This documentation offers comprehensive guidance, featuring sample use cases, reference architectures, design principles, and best practices to support organizations in their cloud adoption journey. Common themes span across these resources, helping organizations understand, implement, and optimize their cloud solutions effectively.

The following pillars are commonly found across these resources, providing a framework for effective cloud design and implementation:

- Reliability: This refers to the ability of a system to consistently and dependably meet its desired outcomes, including high availability, scalability, disaster recovery, and fault tolerance. This encompasses the system's capacity to withstand component failures, network inconsistencies, and other disruptions, ensuring that it remains operational and effective in the face of unexpected events. Reliability is thus a key factor in evaluating a system's overall quality and its ability to maintain its performance, integrity, and availability, even in the presence of potential failures or disruptions.

- Security: This is a fundamental pillar for banking organizations that ensures the system is protected against various types of threats, including distributed denial-of-service attacks, hacking, and cross-site scripting attacks. This also encompasses data security, which involves safeguarding data at rest, in transit, and in use. Additionally, this pillar addresses user and system access permissions, ensuring that only authorized individuals have access to sensitive information. Furthermore, it ensures compliance with relevant regulatory requirements, providing an additional layer of protection against potential vulnerabilities and ensuring the confidentiality, integrity, and availability of sensitive data.
- Cost optimization: Cost optimization in cloud applications relies heavily on selecting the right services and controlling their usage. This involves strategic decisions on selecting cost-effective resources, leveraging available discounts, and accurately estimating the cost of ownership. Effective governance and monitoring of usage are also crucial, as they enable organizations to identify areas of inefficiency and make data-driven decisions to optimize costs. Additionally, implementing budgeting alerts and notifications helps to prevent unexpected cost spikes and ensures that cloud expenses remain within predetermined limits, ultimately leading to a more cost-efficient cloud infrastructure.
- Operational Excellence: Software Operations encompasses the post-production deployment activities that ensure the smooth running, availability, and health of software applications. It involves deploying changes, monitoring performance, and implementing alerting, preventive, and corrective measures to maintain application health. A key aspect of effective Software Operations is automation, which enables the efficient execution of repeated tasks such as code deployments and infrastructure provisioning. Additionally, Software Operations teams must define and meet Service Level Agreements (SLAs) that ensure the quality of service and responsiveness to user needs. By focusing on automation and SLA management, organizations can reduce downtime, improve application performance, and enhance the overall user experience.
- Performance Efficiency: Performance Efficiency is a critical metric that evaluates a system's ability to perform at the desired level, while minimizing waste and maximizing resource utilization. To achieve optimal performance efficiency, organizations must consider a range of factors, including the strategic use of managed services, serverless functions, and databases tailored to specific workloads. Additionally, effective network configurations, data flow restrictions, caching mechanisms, and other technologies are essential for reducing latency, improving throughput, and ensuring reliable system performance. By optimizing performance efficiency, organizations

can reduce costs, enhance user experience, and increase overall system scalability and agility.

These guiding principles serve as a roadmap for designing and implementing effective cloud solutions, providing organizations with in-depth guidance as they embark on their cloud transformation journey. By adhering to these principles, organizations can ensure that their cloud strategies are tailored to their unique needs, goals, and constraints, ultimately leading to successful cloud adoption and long-term success.

Conclusion

In this chapter, we have explored the common challenges that organizations face when building IT solutions, as well as the unique obstacles that arise during the cloud adoption process. Additionally, we have provided an overview of the guiding principles for cloud solutions, which will serve as the foundation for our subsequent discussions.

In the following chapters, we will delve deeper into the design aspects of cloud solutions, specifically focusing on Banking IT Systems and providing practical guidance on how to effectively design and implement cloud-based solutions that meet the unique needs of the banking industry.

References

https://www.linkedin.com/pulse/challenges-finance-industry-india-padmajaya-investments/
https://www.ucfs.net/financial-services-challenges/
https://www.taskus.com/insights/financial-services-industry-challenges/
https://blog.golimelight.com/cfo-central/financial-services-challenges
https://global.hitachi-solutions.com/blog/top-10-challenges-banking-financial-organizations-can-overcome/

Chapter 6
Designing Banking Cloud Solutions

In the previous few chapters of the book, we have understood the basics of cloud computing, and the typical challenges faced by organizations in their cloud journey. In this chapter let's look at how to overcome those challenges and effectively design banking cloud solutions.

Following topics will be covered in this chapter

- Defining the Cloud Migration Strategy
- Guidelines for choosing a suitable cloud offering
- Critical aspects for designing the cloud solution
- Approaches for cloud migration
- Hybrid Solutions

Defining the Cloud Migration Strategy

When transitioning an existing application to the cloud, it's crucial to adopt a distinct strategy compared to developing new applications for the cloud. This process entails collaborating with the inherent technological and functional constraints of the existing application, which is already delivering value to the organization. To ensure a smooth transition, it's vital to devise a well-informed and comprehensive plan that accounts for the application's current features and limitations.

Cloud Migration Strategy is a high-level plan that an enterprise embraces to move its IT solutions to cloud hosting environment(s). It should define why, what, when, how to migrate.

- **Why to migrate**: It is critical that all the employees of the organization understand and appreciate the cultural shift because of the cloud migration.
- **When to migrate**: The strategy should align to and driven by Organization's business priorities and the Technology maturity of the applications.
- **What to migrate**: Define how to prioritize and identify which applications to migrate. Also define which type components (Data / middleware / UI) are suitable for migration.
- **How**: Provide guidelines and roadmaps on assessing the applications, planning for the migration, selecting suitable cloud providers, define the reference cloud architectures and templates, how to execute (tools available for the migration), validate, govern, and optimize.

Based on the assessment, a suitable migration framework needs to be identified for each application. There are 6 popular strategies available called the 6 R's of cloud Migration.

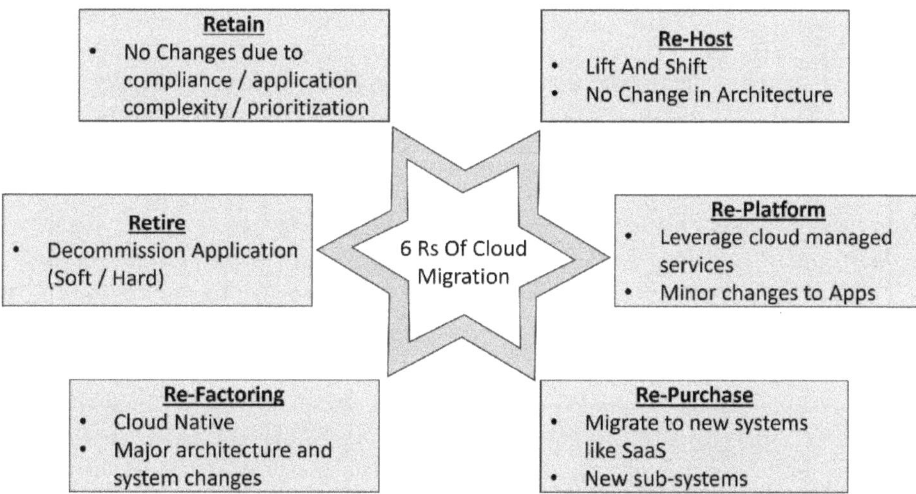

Figure 6.1: 6 R's (Strategies of Cloud Migration)

Re-Host: This is also commonly referred to as 'lift and shift' where applications are moved as-is from existing on-prem environment to the cloud environment.

- Suitable for legacy applications or when the organization is in the initial stages of cloud adaptation and maturity.
- Quick and easy solution. This is a good first step and will help reduce hosting costs.
- No change required in the application architecture or implementation. Only networking and configuration changes may be required.

- Does not leverage full cloud potential and cloud native technologies.

Re-Platform: Here applications are migrated with some optimizations that are suitable to the cloud environment, without changing the core application architecture.

- This will result in increased performance, cost, and effort benefits.
- Leverage cloud managed services like Databases, Application servers, auto-scaling, etc
- Minor application changes will be required to integrate with cloud services.

Re-Purchase: As part of the migration, one or more of the application components are replaced with a different cloud proprietary / opensource / As-A-Service solution.

- Migrate from legacy to cloud-based services.
- Involves implementing and integrating with new sub-systems, requiring technology change.
- Significant changes to the application architecture for the new components.

Re-factoring: Replace the existing solution and implement all or major components of the application using cloud native features like serverless, service oriented, container based, interoperable. This approach is

- Mature cloud adoption strategy to leverage the full potential of cloud computing
- Requires major architecture and system changes
- Aligns with the long-term vision of the organization to move-to-cloud
- Flexible to accommodate business processes and functional changes to add new features.
- Migration involves complete SDLC and is expensive.

Retire: Decommission un-used applications, because of changing business needs or availability of cheaper and efficient alternative COTS products.

- Reduced operational expenditure.
- Can be implemented in a phased manner to soft-decommission (system is turned off) followed by hard-decommission (system components are removed to free up the infrastructure resources)

Retain: Retain the existing application as is. This strategy is suitable for applications in following scenarios:

- Reaching end-of-life soon
- Too complex to migrate due to proprietary software and integration dependencies.
- Compliance restrictions to store and process data.
- De-prioritized for future scope or lack of cloud maturity.

Guidelines for choosing a suitable cloud offering

There are diverse cloud options available from multiple vendors, ensuring a suitable choice for your specific needs. It is advisable to explore all alternatives, potentially combining multiple cloud services, to find the optimal solution. The initial step towards cloud adoption involves evaluating if cloud computing is suitable for your specific scenario. If it is, you will then proceed to select a fitting cloud solution.

When considering cloud implementation, it is common for reducing infrastructure costs to be a significant motivation. However, this should not be the sole factor. Cloud computing offers numerous advantages, such as enhanced security, increased availability, improved scalability, and better efficiency. To maximize these benefits, it is recommended to avoid a big-bang approach and instead adopt a phased approach to implementation, allowing for a more controlled and gradual transition.

Assessing the cloud readiness of your application is crucial before migrating to the cloud. Various tools available in the market can help evaluate your application based on factors like workloads, non-functional requirements (NFR), technology stack, and existing hardware/software. Utilizing these tools early in your cloud journey enables a thorough evaluation of your application's cloud readiness, its potential and the benefits that can be gained.

When selecting a cloud offering, consider the following questions to ensure a suitable fit:

- Is this for migrating an existing application or developing a born-on-the-cloud solution? For cloud-native applications, Platform as a Service (PaaS) is often the best choice due to its quick MVP achievement and incremental functionality implementation. For as-is migration of an existing application, there are are usually limitations on the middleware compatibility (like a specific version of the OS/software), so Infrastructure as a Service (IaaS) could be the right solution.
- When migrating a legacy application to the cloud, verify if the necessary middleware is supported by the cloud offering. Since compatibility issues with middleware can lead to significant changes in the application, it is essential to confirm the availability of the required middleware support before proceeding with the migration. This step can help prevent potential issues and save time and effort during the migration process.
- When selecting a cloud offering, evaluate data security and compliance requirements. Ensure that the chosen cloud option complies with data

regulations and can handle sensitive data, such as personal information or sensitive personal information. Regulatory requirements might prohibit storing sensitive data on a public cloud instance, or there could be geographical restrictions. In such cases, consider a hybrid cloud solution with data on-premises and application services deployed on a public cloud. Also, evaluate the cloud offering based on single tenant versus multi-tenant architecture.

- When selecting a cloud offering, determine if the application is internet-facing or intranet-based. Public or private cloud hosting options differ based on network/firewall configurations. Internet-facing applications can still be hosted behind a firewall using a private cloud. In such cases, an instance of the public cloud can handle external traffic and route it back to the private cloud for processing. In this setup, the public cloud serves as a gateway, exposing the application to the internet, while the private cloud manages the application's business logic and data.
- Consider whether the application requires integration with existing enterprise applications behind the firewall. Public clouds may not be suitable for such applications due to corporate firewall policies and interface maturity. In such cases, a private cloud or a hybrid cloud solution might be more appropriate.
- Determine if the application incorporates any third-party or open-source components. If such dependencies are present, assess their compatibility with the chosen PaaS platform. Should the application rely on unsupported third-party or open-source elements, two options become available: either modify the application to accommodate the selected PaaS platform or replace the problematic dependencies. This approach ensures seamless integration and optimal performance of the application within the chosen PaaS environment.

Critical Aspects for Designing the Cloud Solution

Once the appropriate target cloud environment has been identified, the next step is to design the cloud solution.

The following are the critical aspects to be consider during design:

- **Security**: This is one of the primary deterrents for organizations to adopting cloud solutions and organizations often hesitate to adopt cloud solutions due to security concerns. To ensure appropriate security measures, consider implementing the following:
  - **Security controls**
    - **Deterrent controls**: These are designed to discourage

potential attackers.
- **Preventative controls**: These aim to prevent unauthorized access or attacks from occurring.
- **Detective controls**: These helps identify any security breaches that may have occurred.
- **Corrective controls**: These are put in place to correct any security issues that have been identified.
- **Access controls**
  - **Identity management**: Ensuring that only authorized individuals have access to sensitive information.
  - **Physical security**: Protecting against unauthorized access to physical resources.
  - **Personnel security**: Implementing strict hiring and screening processes to ensure that employees are trustworthy.
  - **Privacy**: Guaranteeing that personal data is handled securely and in compliance with relevant regulations.
- **Data Controls**
  - **Confidentiality**: Ensuring that sensitive data remains confidential and is only accessible to authorized individuals.
  - **Access control**: Implementing measures to control who can access specific data sets.
  - **Integrity**: Ensuring that data remains accurate and consistent over its entire lifecycle.
  - **Encryption**: Implementing encryption for data in transit, data at rest, and data in use is crucial for securing sensitive information. Additionally, encrypting backed-up data is also a vital step in safeguarding this information.
- **Other security considerations**
  - Comply with business continuity and data recovery requirements.
  - Maintain log and audit trails.
  - Address legal and contractual issues when implementing cloud solutions
- **High availability (HA) and disaster recovery (DR)** are critical considerations in cloud hosting, as cloud providers typically have limited control over scheduled and unplanned outages. To ensure minimal downtime and maintain business continuity, robust component design should incorporate HA and DR functionality. The cloud infrastructure itself does not provide these features, but they can be achieved through provider services and application design integration.
  Some strategies for achieving HA and DR include:
  - Hosting the application across multiple cloud data centers.
  - Implementing application monitoring and automated scaling as

needed.
   o   Utilizing containers for dynamic provisioning of services

By incorporating these strategies, organizations can ensure the reliability and resilience of their cloud-based applications. Cloud features like auto scaling help in designing highly available solutions. Scaling can be achieved vertically, by increasing the power of individual servers, or horizontally, by adding more servers to the system. It's important to note that scaling strategies should be carefully evaluated based on the specific needs and requirements of an organization. While vertical scaling can provide a temporary boost, it often has limitations and can become expensive, potentially creating a single point of failure. In contrast, horizontal scaling offers a long-term advantage, allowing resources to be easily added or removed as needed.

However, this requires an additional layer of management like a load balancer to effectively distribute traffic and ensure seamless operations.

- **Load balancing**: Load balancing is a design pattern that caters to both the security and availability concerns. This is a crucial aspect of cloud-based applications, serving two primary purposes. Firstly, it acts as a proxy, shielding backend application servers from direct traffic and protecting them from potential overload. Secondly, it distributes workload evenly across multiple servers, often located in different regions, to ensure optimal performance and scalability. Cloud providers offer a range of load balancing algorithms, including round-robin, min-min, and min-max, among others. It is essential to understand these options and select the most suitable one to ensure seamless application performance and reliability.
- **Data restoration and backup**: Data is critical to any organization, especially in the banking sector. Any data loss will have adverse results. Data loss can happen due to hardware failures like service crashes, natural disasters, etc or due to software failures like clean-up scripts. So, Data Backup and Restore are crucial considerations for cloud-based applications. Cloud providers offer a range of automated backup services which can be leveraged by application teams to ensure business continuity in the event of data loss. By utilizing these services, organizations can create a robust data backup and restore strategy, enabling them to quickly recover their system and minimize downtime in the event of data loss or corruption.
- **Business Continuity and Disaster Recovery**: Define the following recovery NFRs and design the system to meet them.
    - **Recovery-Time-Objective (RTO)**: Maximum acceptable system or data downtime.
    - **Recovery-Point-Objective (RPO)**: Maximum acceptable amount of data loss
    - **Recovery-Level-Objective (RLO)**: Maximum acceptable granularity of data or functionality loss.

Let's consider an example to illustrate the importance of these metrics in disaster recovery planning. A bank is designing its recovery strategy for a critical application that is vulnerable to system crashes. The application is critical to customer experience, and the bank wants to ensure that it is restored to functionality within a certain timeframe.

The Recovery Time Objective (RTO) is the maximum acceptable time it takes to restore the application to its normal state after a disaster. In this case, the RTO is 1 hour, meaning that the bank wants to restore the application to functionality within 1 hour of the system crash. If it takes longer, the bank risks losing customer trust and experiencing negative consequences.

- o **The Recovery Point Objective (RPO)** is the maximum acceptable period of data loss that can occur during a disaster. In this case, the RPO is 15 minutes, meaning that the bank can tolerate losing at most 15 minutes of data before the disaster strikes. If the bank loses more data than this, it will face significant financial implications.
- o **The Recovery Level Objective (RLO)** defines the granularity of the data to be restored. This may sometimes be represented in numbers like RLO = 95% (restore more than 95% of data), or sometime represented as functionality. Restore Web UI, while it is okay to delay Mobile and API interfaces.

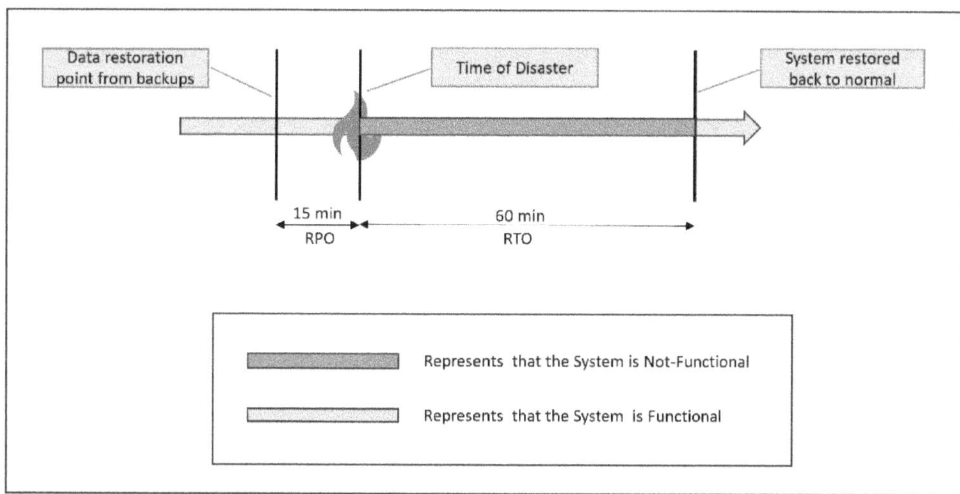

Figure 6.2: Disaster recovery

Say, if a disaster occurs at 4 pm on any given day, then we should be able to recover the data from later than 3:45 pm and the system should be brought up latest by 5pm. For this example, the architecture should include taking backups with a frequency less than 15 min, and the standby system should be made ready within an hour.

- **Use of containers**: Cloud computing's dynamic nature and flexible infrastructure allows for the seamless self-provisioning of processes and memory, making it an ideal environment for containerized architectures like microservices and Docker. With cloud, applications can automatically scale up or down in real-time to accommodate fluctuating workloads, ensuring optimal resource allocation and performance. This flexibility enables the designing of applications to quickly adapt to changing demands, ensuring high availability and responsiveness for users.

- **DevOps pipeline**: Automation is the cornerstone of efficient and reliable software development and deployment. Systems need to behave in a predictable manner in all the environments (dev, test, prod) and issue identification needs to happen in the early phases of the SDLC (shift-left strategy). By leveraging DevOps tools and practices, organizations can streamline repetitive tasks, accelerate deployments, and deliver greater business value to clients. Cloud providers, particularly Platform-as-a-Service (PaaS) solutions, offer a comprehensive suite of DevOps features that enable continuous integration, continuous delivery, continuous deployment, and continuous operations, enabling teams to work more effectively and efficiently.

- **Latency**: In banking solutions, there is usually significant processing involved and requests for transactions traversing multiple systems / sub-systems. This may result in increased latency in delivering the responses. Especially in a hybrid or multi-cloud environment, network latency is a critical factor to consider. There could be multiple network hops involved for a single client request and this may sometimes involve hops potentially across different cloud vendors. Cloud service providers can help minimize latency by intelligently routing end-users to the nearest cloud data center region within their network. This coupled with effective application design not only improves the overall user experience but also ensures efficient resource utilization and cost savings.

Clustered environment: Server clustering refers to the practice of combining multiple resources into a single logical system. This is usually done to improve the performance by increased availability, reliability and scalability of the system. By introducing such redundancies, the system would be more resilient to handle failures in one component by performing seamless failover. This also helps in managing unexpected spikes in the requests by scaling as required. In a clustered setup, it's recommended to assign different servers to separate nodes to ensure high availability. When performing scheduled maintenance, it's best to take one node offline at a time, allowing the remaining nodes to continue serving client requests without interruption. This distributed approach ensures that at least one server remains available to handle requests, minimizing downtime and maintaining system reliability.

The design should also incorporate automated health checks for identifying any failed components to increase resilience, storage replication to maintain data integrity and load balancing for increased availability.

- **Middleware and software**: Applications often rely on a specific set of middleware and software components, which can vary depending on the technology stack. When selecting the best middleware and software for your cloud solution, it's crucial to weigh various factors, including existing application dependencies, available skills, licensing constraints, and the cloud provider's offerings. Cloud vendors typically offer a range of pre-defined options, making it essential to conduct a thorough compatibility assessment before migrating any existing applications. This assessment will help identify potential issues or limitations and ensure that the chosen middleware and software can fully harness the cloud environment's capabilities. In some cases, a partial or complete rewrite of the application may be necessary to unlock the full potential of the cloud and take advantage of its features and capabilities.
- **Monitoring**: To ensure that automated corrective controls are effective, it is essential to establish proper monitoring practices to detect anomalies. This is particularly important for maintaining secure and reliable application and server infrastructure in a cloud environment. Cloud providers offer advanced tools for analyzing virtual machine workloads, providing customizable dashboards and metric collection capabilities that facilitate consolidated monitoring. By utilizing these tools, organizations can implement consistent monitoring practices and configure automated actions to proactively manage system health, such as scaling resources or adjusting service instances, to maintain optimal performance and prevent potential issues.
- **Hybrid cloud solutions**: Integrations between applications operating in different cloud environments, across various vendors, or on-premises require careful planning and configuration. Network security measures, such as firewalls, must be implemented to enable these connections. These integrations can be asynchronous or synchronous, depending on the functional and technical requirements. Caching static data, which does not frequently change, can help reduce application processing times by storing and serving this data more efficiently.

We will discuss designing Hybrid Cloud solutions in detail, later in this chapter. Implementing a cloud solution does not necessarily mean migrating an existing legacy application directly onto shared infrastructure. Although this can be a viable initial step to help decrease infrastructure costs, cloud services provide numerous opportunities for enhancing flexibility and efficiency in a cost-effective manner. Leveraging appropriate services allows organizations to unlock the full potential of the cloud.

Approaches for Cloud Migration

In this section, we will discuss various approaches:

Data Migration and Backups

Banking organizations may encounter situations where they need to migrate their existing data from on-premises data centers to the cloud, either across multiple cloud providers or within the same provider across different regions. Some common scenarios that may necessitate such migrations include:

- Transferring an application and its associated data to the cloud.
- Establishing a Disaster Recovery site to ensure business continuity.
- Creating a backup of critical data to ensure data security and integrity.
- Creating a read-only copy of data to offload process-intensive workloads, such as analytics, reporting, machine learning, and more, from primary systems.

These migrations can be facilitated using various strategies and tools, such as data transfer tools, cloud-to-cloud migration services, and data replication techniques. Organizations should carefully evaluate their specific needs and constraints to determine the most suitable approach for their cloud migration project.

The scope and scale of data migration can vary greatly, depending on the specific requirements and needs of the project. In some cases, the transfer of data may be a one-time event, while in others it may occur in real-time or on a recurring schedule. The amount of data involved can also range significantly, from small amounts in the kilobytes to massive volumes in the petabytes.

The migration solution should be designed to take care of the following factors:

- **Security** – When transmitting data online, it's crucial to ensure secure data transfer, both in transit and at rest. This can be achieved with data encryption and/or network encryption, which scramble the data to prevent unauthorized access. An additional option is to establish a private, dedicated connection for data transfer. Fortunately, many cloud providers offer robust security features, including encryption, to safeguard data stored in their systems (data at rest), providing an added layer of protection against potential threats.
- **Data Integrity** – Ensuring the completeness and consistency of copied data with the original data source is vital. Implementing automated validation mechanisms that meticulously examine the copied data against its source is crucial for identifying and rectifying any discrepancies or errors that might have arisen during the transfer process. By doing so, these mechanisms help

maintain data integrity throughout the migration.

- **Transfer Speed** – Cloud providers often offer a range of services to facilitate data migration, catering to varying data volumes and network speeds. These services may include transferring encrypted data over the public internet, establishing a dedicated private network connection between the on-premises infrastructure and the cloud, as well as providing the option for copying data to an external portable media for physical shipment to the cloud provider.
- **Cost** – Data storage and transfer in the cloud come with associated costs. The amount of data stored incurs a cost, as does the amount of data transferred into and out of the cloud. Notably, most cloud providers offer free ingress, which refers to the transfer of data into the cloud. However, egress, or the transfer of data out of the cloud, typically incurs data transfer charges, which can add up over time.
- **Failed / Partial data transfers** – When migrating large volumes of data over a network, the transfer process can be time-consuming, potentially taking hours or even days to complete. To ensure reliability and minimize downtime, a robust transfer mechanism should be able to handle incremental transfers, allowing for the transfer to resume from where it left off in the event of any interruptions or failures. Where required, data can be split into smaller parts to support parallel transmissions. These features enable the transfer to be restarted quickly, reducing the overall transfer time and minimizing the risk of data loss or corruption.

Application Migration

We have seen the 6R's of Application Migration earlier in this chapter. When discussing the details of application migration strategies, we will concentrate on two approaches that can have substantial consequences for the migration process: Re-Platforming and Re-Factoring. The design approach for these two strategies will be like that of building a cloud-native application from the ground up, ensuring seamless integration and optimal performance in the cloud environment.

Transforming a large, monolithic legacy application into an efficient cloud system requires breaking it down into smaller, manageable services. These services should be container-based, loosely coupled, independently scalable, automatically testable, and capable of rapid deployment. This approach enables a more streamlined and efficient cloud migration process. Before we take a deeper look into the microservices architecture, lets understand the Monolith better.

Historically, software applications have been designed as monolithic structures, comprising a single, large, and complex entity. A classic example is a banking application built using Java and Oracle, which offers various online services to customers, such as account dashboards, profile management, transaction searching, and online money transfers. Initially, this monolithic approach made sense, as all these features were closely related and served a single business need. However, this architecture has its own set of inherent challenges.

- **Scalability**: Each service within a distributed system has unique usage patterns and, consequently, different scalability requirements. For instance, banking application features like viewing recent transactions and accessing the account dashboard are more frequently used in comparison to other features like online money transfers or updating user profiles. However, since the entire application is built as a single, large entity, it becomes quite challenging to independently scale these individual services to meet their unique demands. This can lead to inefficient resource allocation and potential bottlenecks in the system.
- **Slower development cycles**: When introducing new functional changes, the development team must consider the far-reaching implications of their code updates across the entire application. This requires a deep understanding of the complex relationships between various components, leading to slower development cycles and increased risk of introducing errors or bugs. As a result, even minor changes can have a ripple effect, causing unintended consequences and delays in the development process.
- **Reliability**: A small defect in one code segment can have a cascading impact on the entire application, potentially causing widespread issues. This scenario also broadens the scope of testing, requiring comprehensive testing of the entire application, even if only a single component, such as the interest rates calculation module, has undergone a code update. This complexity can lead to longer testing cycles, increased risk of errors, and a higher likelihood of defects propagating throughout the application.
- **Technology constraints**: The example application mentioned above is built using Java and Oracle, which means that all its modules are constrained by the technology's limitations. This lack of flexibility means that if a particular module would benefit from being implemented using a NoSQL data store, that option is not available due to the rigid technology stack. As a result, the application's architecture and design are heavily influenced by the chosen technology, restricting the potential for innovation and adaptability.
- **Complex deployments**: The application is constructed and deployed as a unified whole, thereby elevating deployment risks and intricacy. This necessitates comprehensive planning for the go-live and recovery processes, ensuring minimal disruption and a smooth transition.
- **Growing Technical Debt**: As the business requirements evolve over time, new features get integrated into the existing codebase, leading to an increase

in size and complexity. When multiple developers are involved in modifying the code, they may hesitate to alter the existing code to minimize the risk of unintentionally disrupting existing functionality. This behavior can result in the accumulation of stale and unused or "orphaned" code within the application, which in turn contributes to the buildup of Technical Debt. Technical Debt refers to the implied cost of additional rework caused by choosing an easy (and potentially less optimal) solution now instead of using a better approach that would take longer.

Microservice architecture offers a solution to address complex challenges by breaking down an application into smaller, independent services. Each service can be developed, deployed, and managed separately, allowing for greater flexibility and autonomy. This approach also enables polyglot programming, where different services can be built using the most suitable technology stack for their specific purpose. For instance, a reporting service could be built using a framework like Tableau, which is optimized for creating reports and dashboards, while complex transaction processing can still be done using Java.

In the microservice architecture, each service is treated as an individual module, overseen by a self-reliant team. Automation is crucial for the success of this pattern, as it streamlines the process of building, testing, deploying, and monitoring these services. Implementing this pattern necessitates a shift in culture and technological understanding, so it should be introduced gradually, allowing teams to adapt and optimize their processes over time. By following this approach, organizations can reap the benefits of microservices while minimizing potential disruptions and risks associated with rapid transformation.

When transitioning to microservices architecture, it's essential to approach the migration with a clear strategy to ensure a successful outcome. This involves adopting a range of supporting tools and practices, including exposing services as APIs, designing loose coupling between services, using containerization to make them self-sufficient, implementing service discovery, enabling inter-service communication, centralizing logging and monitoring, and automating DevOps processes. By carefully planning and executing these components, organizations can effectively navigate the complexity of microservices and reap its benefits.

Hybrid solutions

In the previous chapter, 'Introduction to Cloud Computing', we covered the various Cloud Deployment Models. For many banking organizations, a Hybrid cloud approach has emerged as the most suitable solution to meet their specific needs. In this section, we will delve deeper into the Hybrid model, examining its benefits, challenges, and best practices, to provide a comprehensive understanding of how it can be leveraged to optimize cloud adoption in the banking sector.

Enterprises often utilize a diverse range of IT applications, each built using various technologies and possessing unique non-functional requirements. Furthermore, these applications frequently rely on and integrate with different internal and external services. In the banking sector, where data handling and compliance regulations are particularly stringent, it is essential to adopt a flexible approach to mitigate potential risks. Rather than relying solely on a single hosting environment, a hybrid approach that combines multiple environments, tailored to meet the specific needs of each application, can provide a more effective and secure solution.

A Hybrid Cloud is a cloud computing environment where applications run on more than one set of distributed computing resources. This is usually a combination of on-premises, private and public cloud solutions integrated seamlessly into single environment. As the IT solutions grow, they become complex and Hybrid Cloud Computing environment provides increased flexibility in choosing the appropriate hosting options that cater to the business needs.

Key Benefits of Hybrid Cloud is that it provides great flexibility for running their workloads - Banks can chose a combination of environment(s) that best suit their requirements. Different systems within the enterprise may leverage different Hybrid cloud components and design. This will help the organization meet its Performance, Resiliency, Scalability, and Compliance requirements while helping to manage the cost.

Hybrid cloud solutions come with their own set of unique challenges:

- Complex integration solution resulting in compatibility issues between the components as there are many moving discrete heterogeneous parts.
- The solution relies on distributed systems, and this increases the number of failure points.
- This also introduces security risks in the systems as each component is dependent on other remote components for data and / or services.
- Each component of the overall solutions is dependent on reliable and efficient network connectivity. This will require designing the solution to handle network failures and latencies.
- Administrative and operational overhead to distributed subsystems and environments that are managed by different vendors.

Best practices for designing an efficient Hybrid Cloud Infrastructure:

- **Use open-source** and platform neutral technologies where suitable. This will increase the portability of the solution, and components can easily be migrated to a different provider if required.
- **Data Handling**: It is a preferred approach to store confidential data on-prem or private cloud, where the banking enterprises have more control. The data backups can then be encrypted and stored in a less expensive cloud storage.
- **Regulatory and compliance restrictions like GDPR** need to be taken into consideration when storing and processing data. There may be restrictions on where the data is stored, how it is stored and where it is accessed from. These requirements can be met by leveraging appropriate cloud services and features.
- **Managing clustered infrastructure** for High Availability and Disaster recovery. The design needs to be able to handle the availability and fail-over requirements based on the criticality of the solution.
- Take advantage of public cloud capabilities to run resource-intensive, temporary, or irregular workloads, which can benefit from the scalability and flexibility offered by the cloud. Additionally, public clouds provide extensive support for popular libraries and frameworks, such as machine learning, allowing developers to easily integrate these technologies into their applications.
- Lower environments like Development and Testing can rely on public cloud hosting. If there are concerns around data handling on cloud, data should be cleansed and masked before storing in cloud.

Like a Hybrid Cloud Environment, A Multi-Cloud strategy involves leveraging a combination of services from multiple public cloud providers, such as Google, AWS, IBM Cloud, Oracle Cloud and Azure, to create a diverse cloud ecosystem. This approach is particularly beneficial when organizations seek to mitigate dependence on a single cloud provider and avoid vendor lock-in, thereby ensuring greater flexibility, resilience, and cost-effectiveness. By utilizing multiple cloud services, organizations can better manage risk, optimize resource allocation, and stay ahead of the competition.

Conclusion

In this chapter we have seen how to design effective banking cloud solutions by defining the Cloud Migration Strategy, understanding the guidelines for choosing a suitable cloud offering and the various approaches for cloud migration. In the next chapter we will take a deep-dive and look at more advanced aspects of the design, discuss best practices and some reference cloud migration use-cases.

Chapter 7
Designing Cloud Solutions – Deep Dive

In the previous chapter, we examined the high-level components of a cloud migration strategy, explored essential recommendations for selecting the optimal cloud solution and overview of the design principles. As we delve deeper into this chapter, we will build upon the foundation established earlier.

Here, we will focus on the intricate technical aspects of designing cloud solutions and exploring best practices and essential considerations to ensure a smooth and efficient transition. Following are the topics covered in this chapter:

- Understanding the range of cloud offerings
- Design Best Practices
- Reference Use cases
- Banking Industry Architecture Network (BIAN)

Understanding the range of cloud offerings

Cloud providers offer a diverse array of services that can often address a broad range of use cases. To ensure successful cloud adoption, it is essential to comprehend the scope of cloud offerings, enabling you to select the most suitable services that align with your specific requirements.

In this section, we will explore the common services that cloud providers typically offer, providing a foundation for informed decision-making in your cloud migration journey.

Geographical hosting Options: Cloud hosting locations are strategically dispersed across the globe to ensure business continuity, provide fast and reliable access to applications, and comply with regional regulatory requirements.

This widespread distribution helps to mitigate the risk of service disruptions caused by natural disasters, while also enabling users to access cloud services with minimal latency and reduced reliance on a single location.

- **Regions**: A region in the cloud refers to a geographically distinct location, usually spread across the globe. They are designed to meet specific regulatory requirements or serve specific geographic markets. Data transfer between regions, however, may incur additional costs and increase the latency.
- **Zones**: A zone is a group of geographically proximate data centers within a region, offering co-location and high-speed connectivity between facilities. Although data centers within a zone are physically separated, they are connected via a low-latency network, enabling fast and efficient data transfer between them.

Compute Services: Compute Services in the cloud enable the execution of applications, offering a range of hardware and software options to support the specific requirements of each workload.

- **Compute (Infrastructure-as-a-service)** Cloud providers offer a range of optimization options for compute resources, allowing you to tailor your infrastructure to meet the specific needs of your application. This includes choices for CPU and memory capacity, as well as networking configurations.
- **Container Solutions**: Container as a Service (CaaS) is a cloud-based offering that enables the orchestration and management of containerized applications, providing a scalable and efficient way to deploy, manage, and scale container-based solutions.
- **Serverless Computing (Function-as-a-Service)**: This is a highly scalable, modular environment for running individual functions, without need to provision or manage underlying infrastructure. This usually supports common programming languages like Java, Python, etc.

Storage Services: There are a wide range of services available to cater for different types of data storage needs.

- **Block Storage**: This is a high-performance storage solution that provides low-latency access to data, typically attached directly to compute instances. This storage option can be categorized into two types: local storage and network storage. Local storage is physically attached to the instance, providing ephemeral storage that is lost when the instance is terminated. Network storage, on the other hand, is a durable and persistent solution that allows data to be stored and retrieved over a network, providing a high level of availability and durability.

- **File Storage**: File storage is a network-based storage solution that provides a POSIX (Portable Operating System Interface) compliant interface for managing and accessing files.
- **Object storage**: Object storage is a scalable and cost-effective solution for storing a wide range of unstructured data, including binary files, videos, audio files, and text documents. This type of storage is very cheap and is particularly well-suited for long-term data archiving and is often used for purposes such as data backup, disaster recovery, and data retention. Object storage provides multiple storage classes, each tailored to specific data usage requirements, and offers advanced features like automatic object migration, data retention policies, versioning, and delete locking.
- **Relational Databases**: Relational databases are well-suited for storing data with a predefined schema, providing a structured environment for managing and analyzing data. They offer two primary use cases: Online Transaction Processing (OLTP) for handling high-volume, high-velocity transactions, and Online Analytics Processing (OLAP) for complex analytics and reporting.
- **No SQL Databases**: NoSQL databases are designed for high-performance data storage and retrieval, often in environments where data structures are not rigidly defined or where schema flexibility is required. This makes them particularly well-suited for big data, real-time web applications, and other use cases where data is constantly changing or evolving.
- **Data Warehouse**: A data warehouse is a centralized repository designed to store and manage massive amounts of data, providing a scalable and efficient platform for running business intelligence (BI) applications, such as reporting and data analytics. By consolidating data from multiple sources, a data warehouse enables organizations to gain insights, make data-driven decisions, and optimize business operations.
- **Data Lake solutions**: A data lake is a centralized, scalable, and flexible repository that enables the ingestion, processing, and storage of enterprise-wide data, regardless of its structure, format, or source. This provides a comprehensive set of tools and technologies to handle large volumes of data, allowing organizations to store and manage their data in its native format, and then process and analyze it as needed.
- **CDN and In-Memory data stores**: A Content Delivery Network (CDN) is a distributed system that stores static content at edge locations around the world, closer to users. This helps to reduce latency and improve page load times, resulting in faster and more efficient content delivery.
- **In-memory data stores**, on the other hand, are designed to cache frequently accessed data at the server side, providing quick and easy access to this data. This can help reduce the time it takes to retrieve and process data by the server.

Data Processing: as below

- **ETL**: Extract, Transform, and Load processing pipelines are designed to handle both batch and streaming data, enabling organizations to extract data from various sources, transform it into a usable format, and load it into a target system or database.
- **Data Preparation**: Data preparation involves cleaning, transforming, and preparing data to meet the requirements of the target service. This process is particularly important when data is received from external sources. This process may also involve masking sensitive information, such as personal identifiable information (PII), to ensure compliance with data security and privacy regulations.
- **Analytics and visualization**: These tools enable organizations to analyze data using custom algorithms and present the insights in a visually appealing and easy-to-understand format through dashboards. These tools provide a platform for data scientists and analysts to explore complex data sets, identify patterns and trends, and create interactive reports and dashboards that facilitate data-driven decision-making.
- **Machine Learning**: ML environments, offered by cloud providers, empower data scientists to train, deploy, and manage machine learning models at scale. These environments provide a range of pre-built models and algorithms, such as image and video recognition, speech-to-text conversion, natural language processing, and more.

Security: as below

- **Data Encryption**: Cloud-based encryption solutions provide secure data at rest by using generated keys or customer-provided keys. These keys are stored in a secure vault, which offers a range of life-cycle management activities, including automatic key rotation, to ensure the highest level of security and compliance.
- **IAM**: Identity and Access Management (IAM) is a feature that controls and restricts access to cloud resources. With IAM, organizations can define granular policies that specify which users, groups, or roles can perform specific actions on specific resources, from specific locations, and at specific times. Additionally, IAM services can seamlessly integrate with existing user repositories, such as Active Directory, and manage access to distributed resources across hybrid cloud environments, providing a single pane of glass for identity and access management.
- **Network Layer**: Network Security can be effectively implemented by combining various services and strategies. This includes:
    - **Logical Grouping and Isolation**: Utilizing Virtual Private Clouds (VPCs) and Subnets to segment the network and restrict access to specific resources. This will be discussed in-depth in the Networking Section of this chapter.

- o **Access Control**: Configuring Firewall rules to regulate data flow between resources by allowing or denying traffic from specific IP addresses. Additionally, Gateways can be set up to manage internet traffic.
- o **Real-time Monitoring**: Configuring Network Flow logs to monitor data transmission in real-time, enabling proactive and reactive measures to be taken as needed.

By leveraging these services and strategies, organizations can ensure the security and integrity of their networks, protecting against unauthorized access and data breaches.

Devops: DevOps (Development – Operations) is a software development and delivery methodology that combines the principles of development and operations to facilitate the rapid and reliable delivery of software. By leveraging a set of practices and tools, DevOps enables organizations to automate and streamline the software delivery lifecycle, ensuring predictability, reliability, and efficiency.

- **Continuous Integration**: This is a software development practice that involves automatically building, testing, and packaging software code on a regular basis, typically after each commit or merge of code into the source code repository. This process includes a range of automated tasks, such as compiling of code, unit testing, building the deplorables, static-code-analysis, security scanning etc. This enables developers to detect and address errors early on, ensuring that the software is reliable, stable, and meets the required quality standards.
- **Continuous Deployment**: Continuous Deployment (CD) is a software development practice that involves automatically deploying software code to test environments on a regular basis, typically after each successful build. This process includes automated deployment of software, configuration, executing regression, and integrated testing. This enables organizations to rapidly deploy software changes to test environments, ensuring that the software is thoroughly tested and validated before being released to production, thereby reducing the associated risks.
- **Continuous Delivery**: This is a software development practice that involves automatically deploying software code to production environments on a regular basis, typically after each successful validation in the Test environments. This may sometimes require including manual approval steps for critical requirements. By automating these tasks, CD enables organizations to rapidly deliver software changes to production environments. There are multiple deployment strategies like rolling, canary, blue green, etc. to deliver software.
- **Continuous Testing**: This is a software development practice that involves continuously testing and monitoring all components of an application,

including software, hardware, networking, and other dependencies. This approach ensures that the application is thoroughly tested and validated throughout its SDLC, and that any issues or anomalies are detected, alerted and addressed promptly. This also provides feedback via dashboards.

- **Continuous Operation**: This practice ensures the reliability and availability of a system. It involves taking automated actions, both preventive and corrective, to identify and address any anomalies that may impact the system's performance or availability. These automated actions can include auto-scaling, fallback, taking backups and snapshots, provided degraded performance, etc. This topic is explained further in the 'Operations effectiveness' section later in this chapter.
- **Infrastructure-as-a-Code**: This is a methodology that enables the automation of infrastructure provisioning and configuration management through code. This approach involves writing code to infrastructure provisioning (define and provision the infrastructure resources, such as hardware, including compute, storage, and networking), as well as configuration management (configuring the installed software and components on these provisioned resources). This helps to reduce the risk of errors, improve efficiency, and increase the speed and agility of infrastructure deployment and management.

System Integration: This is the process of combining multiple components, subsystems, and external systems within a software solution to create a seamless and cohesive whole.

- **Asynchronous Integration**: Asynchronous Integration is a type of integration where components communicate with each other in an asynchronous manner, allowing for greater flexibility, scalability, and reliability. In this approach, the message provider and consumer are decoupled, meaning they are isolated from each other and can operate independently.
- There are two primary types of Asynchronous Integration Message Queues (a one-to-one integration where a single publisher sends messages to a single subscriber) and Publish-Subscribe (a one-to-many integration where a single publisher sends messages to multiple subscribers who can register for specific topics or messages). In both cases, messages can be ordered, and duplicates can be eliminated, ensuring that the integration is efficient and reliable.
- **Synchronous Integration**: This is a type of integration where components communicate with each other in real-time, with the caller making a blocking call to the service provider and waiting for a response. The response would usually be a success / failure / time-out. Synchronous Integration is typically achieved over HTTP/HTTPS using REST (Representational State Transfer) or SOAP (Simple Object Access Protocol) protocols. This approach is suitable for applications that require a direct and immediate response from

the service provider, and where the caller can afford to wait for the response.
- **Service Mesh**: This is a layer that sits between microservices and provides a set of features to manage and orchestrate their communication. This layer is responsible for managing the interactions between services, ensuring that they can communicate effectively and efficiently. Some of the key features that a Service Mesh provides include service discovery, load balancing, traffic management, security, etc. This helps to simplify the complexity of microservice communication, improve the reliability and scalability of services, and reduce the overhead of manual configuration and management

Networking: as below
- **VPC**: A Virtual Private Cloud is a secure and isolated network that allows multiple cloud resources to be grouped together, enabling communication between them without the need for traffic to traverse the public internet. Components within a VPC can be distributed globally, yet still communicate with each other using internal IP addresses, ensuring secure and private communication.
- The VPC provides a virtualized network environment that can be configured to meet specific security and connectivity requirements. Traffic flowing in and out of the network can be monitored and logged, providing visibility into network activity and allowing for easier troubleshooting and security monitoring. In addition, multiple VPCs can be configured to be shared, enabling seamless communication and traffic flow between them. This allows for greater flexibility and scalability in cloud deployments, while also maintaining the security and isolation of each VPC
- **Subnets**: A Subnet is a logical grouping of network resources that enables isolation and organization of network components. Subnets are typically used to separate publicly accessible resources from privately accessible resources, ensuring that sensitive data and applications remain secure.
- Subnets can be configured to control traffic flow by assigning suitable CIDR (Classless Inter-Domain Routing) blocks, which define the range of IP addresses available within the subnet. This allows for granular control over which resources can communicate with each other and which traffic can be allowed to flow in and out of the subnet. Firewall rules can also be used to further restrict traffic flow, ensuring that only authorized traffic is allowed to enter or exit the subnet. This adds an additional layer of security and helps to prevent unauthorized access to sensitive resources.
- Let's take an example to illustrate these concepts better. Imagine a simple banking application built using a three-tier architecture, comprising a web server hosting the user interface, an application server handling the business logic, and a backend database storing the data. To ensure secure communication, we want to restrict internet access to only the web UI layer, while allowing requests to flow smoothly between the layers within a private

network.

- To achieve this, we can group the resources in each layer logically by a VPC. This enables us to assign a range of internal IP addresses for the resources in the network, which can span across multiple Availability Zones for high availability. To isolate publicly accessible resources (web servers) from private resources (application and database servers), we can create separate public and private subnets for each set of resources. We can then control traffic entering each subnet using gateways and firewall rules. For instance, the private subnet can only accept traffic from the public subnet, and not from external sources like the internet or other resources in the same Availability Zone. If there's a further requirement to share resources between two VPCs and send traffic between them using an internal network, we can group the two VPCs as trusted peers. This allows for secure communication and resource sharing between the two networks.

Load Balancing: A Load Balancer is a key component in network architectures that enables efficient and secure distribution of traffic to multiple backend services. Its primary functions include Routing traffic, Load distribution, providing a Single point of entry, Security by inspecting and restricting traffic and Monitoring. Load balancers can be global (managing global traffic across multiple regions or datacenters) or local (managing local traffic within a region or datacenter). In addition, Load Balancers can be classified based on the network layer they operate at - Transport layer (Layer 4, to handle TCP/UDP traffic) and Application Layer (Layer 7, to handle HTTP / HTTPS requests).

API Gateway: APIs are software services exposed by an internal or external provider that can be consumed by clients. An API Gateway is a managed service that acts as a layer between the API services and the client, abstracting away the management complexity from the business services. The API Gateway offers a range of features, including Authentication and authorization, Data encryption, Security offloading (converting HTTPS to HTTP traffic), Path-based routing to backend services, Version control, Caching of static content, Rate limiting (restricting the number of requests from a set of clients), Error handling, Health checks of backend services, Logging and monitoring of traffic flowing through. This allows for a more scalable, secure, and maintainable API architecture. By offloading these functions to the API Gateway, developers can focus on building business logic and services.

As we can see above, cloud providers offer a wide range of services for architects to choose from, depending on the individual needs for the applications.

Design Best Practices

In the previous section, we examined the various services provided by cloud providers. Now, let's delve into the best practices for designing cloud IT solutions while effectively utilizing these services.

- **Prioritize the applications**: For banking organizations with existing IT infrastructure or developing new systems, creating a holistic cloud migration strategy is paramount. This strategy should encompass short-term and long-term objectives regarding application migration to the cloud. The process involves meticulously evaluating applications, categorizing them based on factors like business priorities, cloud maturity, and technology stack compatibility, and devising a phased migration plan for each category. This approach enables a systematic and efficient transition to the cloud while optimizing resources and minimizing disruptions.
- **Validate the feasibility** of the design and the decisions via executing Proof-Of-Concept (POC). Before embarking on a cloud migration, it's crucial to assess the viability of the strategy to ensure it aligns with the organization's readiness. If the organization is still in the early stages of cloud adoption, a thorough validation process is necessary to guarantee success. Based on the findings from analysis and proof-of-concept (POC) testing, the cloud adoption strategy should be reviewed and adjusted as needed to ensure a smooth and effective transition to the cloud.
- Not all applications need a similar architecture: Given the outcomes of previous migration efforts, organizations may be inclined to adopt a uniform approach for all subsequent migrations. However, it's essential to recognize that there is no one-size-fits-all architecture that can effectively support all solutions. Instead, each migration should be treated as a unique case, requiring a customized approach tailored to the specific needs and requirements of the project. A one-size-fits-all approach can lead to inefficiencies, increased risk, and decreased success rates.
- Take an incremental approach for complex applications. While it's tempting to migrate an entire application at once, a big-bang approach is not always the most effective or practical strategy. Instead, a phased migration approach can be taken, allowing for a more measured and controlled transition. This can involve re-hosting certain components or implementing a hybrid approach, which can be a safer and more manageable starting point.
- **Follow SDLC life cycle**: The cloud migration process should be treated as a distinct project with its own set of phases, mirroring the traditional Software Development Life Cycle (SDLC). This includes Assessment, Plan, Requirement identification, Analysis to identify any application / infrastructure changes, Execute and Test. Additionally, depending on the organization's business needs, functional changes can be incorporated into the application as part of the migration process, ensuring that the new cloud-based solution meets the

desired requirements.

- Have a back-out plan. When developing a migration plan, it's crucial to incorporate a back-out strategy to ensure that the organization can recover in the event of a failure. This contingency plan should outline the steps to be taken in case of a partial or complete failure during the migration process.
- After the migration exercise is complete, a go/no-go decision should be made to assess the success or failure of the activity. If the outcome is deemed unsuccessful, a fix-forward or roll-back approach should be determined. Fix-forward refers to identifying and addressing the root cause of the failure, while roll-back involves reverting back to the previous state or a previous version that was known to be stable.
- Plan for any data loss and application downtime: During the data migration process, it's essential to acknowledge the possibility of data loss and take proactive measures to mitigate this risk. This includes incorporating data integrity checks as part of the validation activity to ensure the accuracy and completeness of the migrated data.
- The application migration activity will involve multiple implementations, cut-over steps, and integrations with various applications and services, requiring coordination with multiple internal and external parties. To ensure a smooth and successful deployment, a suitable deployment pattern should be followed, such as blue-green or canary deployments.
- A detailed implementation runbook should be created to guide the execution of the deployment, outlining the steps, timelines, and responsible parties involved. This runbook will help ensure that the deployment is executed accurately and efficiently, minimizing the risk of errors and downtime
- **Usage of Managed Services**: Managed services involve cloud providers managing and maintaining specific services, such as databases, compute, networking, monitoring, and security. By transferring the responsibilities of installations, updates, and maintenance to the cloud provider, application teams can focus on configuring these services according to their unique requirements. This setup allows teams to prioritize building applications and optimizing managed services to create greater business value.
- **Cost Management and Estimation**: Before embarking on a cloud journey, it is crucial to evaluate the Total Cost of Ownership (TCO) associated with migrating to the cloud. This encompasses the expenses of cloud services, human resources, and external services not directly related to the cloud (such as networking, setting up internet and maintaining on-premises infrastructure). Awareness of potential discounts, like continued usage and committed usage discounts, is important to keep the costs down. Post-implementation, cost management can be effectively maintained through the utilization of automation tools, such as monitoring, budgeting alerts, and others, to ensure financial sustainability.
- **Access Security**: Implement the following best practices to enhance security:

- o Avoid sharing of accounts between individuals or systems. Instead, each user or component should have their own account.
- o Grant access to resources based on roles (individuals) or service accounts (components) only.
- o Adhere to the Principle of Least Privilege by providing only the minimum level of access necessary to perform job functions.
- o Ensure Separation of Duties by defining specific roles for each activity, limiting the possibility of fraudulent activities.
- o Implement fine-grained access controls to monitor and track access to cloud resources.
- **Network Security**: To protect against DDoS (Distributed Denial-of-Service) and other OWASP attacks, implement the following countermeasures:
  - o Utilize Firewall Rules to restrict traffic to and from cloud resources.
  - o Minimize the attack surface by limiting the number of services exposed to external networks, maximizing the use of internal IP addresses.
  - o For compliance reasons, opt for single-tenant nodes that provide dedicated hardware features.
- **Quicker system startup:** Reduce component startup time by utilizing reusable templates and hardened custom images. Pre-defined configurations in templates enable quick and consistent instance creation, while pre-built images contain all necessary software, hardware, and configurations, ensuring reliable and rapid deployment of new instances.
- **Automation**: Automate repetitive tasks using tools and templates for Continuous Integration, Continuous Deployment, and Continuous Delivery DevOps pipelines. Configuration and minimal coding are sufficient to achieve this. Additionally, Infrastructure-as-a-Code enables automated infrastructure provisioning and management, offering predictable and repeatable configurations that can be version-controlled for enhanced management and collaboration.
- **Handling Excess Loads**: Anticipate failures and include network and infrastructure in testing. Implement the following strategies to address excess and unpredictable network traffic loads:
  - o **Load shedding**: Temporarily stops traffic to backend services.
  - o **API limits**: Distribute service-level agreements (SLAs) differently for various customer groups, such as paid and free accounts.
  - o **Reduce quality of service**: Route requests to static content when the backend service is unresponsive.
  - o **Leverage loose coupling**: Utilize asynchronous communication to backend services for improved resilience.
- **Deployment strategies**: When it comes to deploying applications, there are various strategies to consider, each with its own advantages and disadvantages. These strategies include gradual deployments, rolling

updates, canary releases, blue-green deployments, and more. Select the most suitable deployment strategy based on the following considerations:
- o Minimizing application downtime.
- o Performing incremental changes.
- o Testing with a subset of users (traffic splitting).
- o Infrastructure cost.
- o Ease of rollback to an earlier stable version.
- **Auto Scaling**: When possible, resources should be configured for autoscaling to ensure optimal performance, scalability and efficient resource utilization. This involves fine-tuning various settings, including:
  - o Minimum and maximum instance counts: defining the range of instances that can be provisioned to handle changing workload demands
  - o Maximum unavailable instances: specifying the maximum number of instances that can be unavailable due to maintenance or other reasons.
  - o Maximum surge: configuring the maximum number of instances that can be increased at a given time to handle sudden spikes in demand.
  - o Cold start considerations: allowing applications to load completely before performing health checks to ensure accurate monitoring and maintenance
- **Disaster recovery and service restoration**: Ensuring the availability of a system is crucial, but the design must balance this requirement with the Non-Functional Requirements (NFRs) and associated costs. To achieve this balance, it's essential to define three key availability metrics:
  - o Recovery Time Objective (RTO): Maximum acceptable application downtime.
  - o Recovery Point Objective (RPO): Maximum acceptable period of data loss.
  - o Recovery Level Objective (RLO): Maximum scope of service loss, such as the granularity of data restored (e.g., restoration of at least 95% of user data)
- **Operations effectiveness**: Monitor resource health effectively using the following tools and techniques:
  - o Inspect application logs, audit logs, and trace data for insights.
  - o Establish robust alerting and visualization (dashboard) mechanisms to handle issues.
  - o Store, retain, and audit logs for future analysis.
  - o Implement automated corrective actions, such as restarting failed instances, adjusting autoscaling based on traffic load, blocking suspicious network traffic, and limiting request volume according to service-level agreements (SLAs).
  - o Reduce quality of service, like providing static content, and

implementing retry strategies with exponential backoff.

In the next section, let's have a look at sample use-cases for reference.

Reference Use cases

After examining the various service options available on the cloud and discussing best practices for cloud adoption, let's now apply our knowledge to real-world scenarios. We'll explore a few reference use-cases that demonstrate how to identify a suitable cloud migration option and the strategies to support our cloud journey. This hands-on approach will help solidify our understanding of cloud computing and prepare us to tackle more complex projects in the future.

Migrating Legacy Mainframe applications.

Use case: A Bank is working on their Cloud adoption roadmap. They have a legacy Mainframe Application that has a high business critical value.

Analysis:

- The application has been in existence for a couple of decades.
- There is minimal or no documentation available and the business rules are embedded inside the application.
- There are few application SMEs who have been with the application since the inception and are considered as critical resources.
- The application is quite stable and hardly requires any changes or maintenance.

Migration Options:

Option	Pros	Cons
1. Retain	The application is stable for many years now. Owing to the complexity and lack of any documentation of the application, it is considered risky to migrate.	The application is critical for the business and is supported by very few critical resources. Technology is outdated and there are performance implications. The application is not extensible and new features are usually avoided.

Option	Pros	Cons
2. Refactor	Leverage new technology features. Business functionality can be made extensible, to easily adapt to the dynamic industry needs.	Lack of documentation makes the migration laborious and time consuming.

Table 7.1: Migration options

Preferred Approach: **Refactor**

- The application should be refactored owing to the dependencies and growing technology debt.
- There are several tools available in the market that can assist by ingesting the legacy code to generate documentation and generate corresponding code for modern technologies like java.
- The generated documentation should be validated and enriched by business SMEs. This will form the basis to capture the requirements and identify corresponding test-cases.
- The plan should be to incrementally modernize the system by breaking it down into smaller, logical modules. This will reduce the risk and enables thorough testing of the new application.
- The scope should be limited to migrating the functionality as-is and It is best to avoid including any new-functionality. Functional changes can be taken up in subsequent phases, once the migrated system stabilizes.

Migrating Legacy Java application

Use case: A Bank has a legacy Java monolith application. The application has been growing over the years and getting difficult to manage. The database is an RDBMS hosted on-prem dedicated servers.

Analysis:

- The application was built using initial versions of Java a few years back when the bank came into existence.
- The application is a typical web-based three-tier architecture using MVC (Modal-View-Controller) framework.
- There are frequent enhancements and functionality changes to be implemented with the changing business needs and technology and infrastructure upgrades.
- The organization is looking at migrating the application to cloud and simultaneously transition to an API based microservice solution.
- For compliance reasons, the data needs to reside on the Bank's premise and should be processed within the geography.

Migration Options:

Option	Pros	Cons
Rehosting	• No changes required to the application. Easy and quick approach	• Will not be leveraging the full potential of the cloud features. • The application is in the path of modernization. So rehosting is extra effort.
Re-Platform	• The application is built using distributed technologies and has been upgraded to use the new versions of the technology stack. So, it should be compatible with the cloud hosting, like containerizing the existing application, with minimal or no changes to the application code.	• Data cannot be migrated to cloud due to the compliance reasons, so it will result in complex integration with on-premises Database.
Refactor	• Results in more scalable, adaptable, flexible, extensible solution	• Considerable change in the architecture. • Needs new technology skills to achieve this exercise.

Table 7.2: Migration options (refactor)

<u>Preferred Approach</u>: **Re-Platform** as an immediate solution with **Refactoring** as a long-term strategic solution

- Consideration: The DB needs to remain on-prem for compliance reasons. So, this requires an Hybrid Cloud approach with the middleware hosted on cloud, that integrates with the on-premise Database.
- Since the application is using the latest technology stack, it can be easily re-platformed into a container-based solution on cloud, to enable leveraging features like scalability, flexibility in deployment options, etc. This should be achievable with minimal or no changes to the application code.
- As a long-term strategic solution, the application should be incrementally modernized into a microservices based architecture.

Migrating Document Storage system

<u>Use case</u>: A Bank has a custom-built document management system, to store and manage all its bank documents.

<u>Analysis:</u>

- The document management system is custom built by the bank and is supported by a dedicated team.
- New features are difficult to implement and test.
- The storage is becoming unmanageable and untraceable, often resulting in duplicate documents being uploaded. It also gets difficult to search for and find documents when required.
- Most of the commonly used features like automated backups are managed by custom scripts.

<u>Migration Options:</u>

Option	Pros	Cons
Repurchase	• Many COTS products and SaaS solutions are available that are easy to manage and provide lot more customization. • These solutions usually come with their migration tools to help migrate existing documents to the tool.	
Retain	• Since the processes are already automated using shell scripts, they may not be required to be modernize.	• The solution is difficult to manage due to the ever-growing size. • Slow in implementing any new features and is an arduous task.

Table 7.3: Migration options –document storage

<u>Preferred Approach</u>: **Repurchase**: Migrate to a suitable COTS solution like 'box' to manage the documents.

- Cost effective solution than the existing one.
- Provides many easy to use, modern features.
- Tools available for seamless migration.

Banking Industry Architecture Network (BIAN)

BIAN (Banking Industry Architecture Network, (https://bian.org/) is a collaborative effort among banks, third-party solution providers, and other industry members aimed at establishing a semantic framework for promoting interoperability in banking services. Established in 2008, BIAN serves as an independent, non-profit association fostering collaboration among its members to develop and maintain a standardized framework for seamless integration of banking services.

Historically, banking IT systems were developed on legacy platforms, which evolved over time and grew increasingly complex. These systems often featured proprietary business logic, with applications developed in isolation. As a result, banks transitioned from building individual applications to constructing IT services, aiming for greater interoperability and reusability. Simultaneously, the growing interconnectedness of banks necessitated the use of common languages, particularly when services were shared across organizational boundaries.

BIAN's primary objective is to create a semantic framework for banking services that emphasizes interface definition (the 'what') to improve interoperability and accelerate global adoption. The focus is not on service implementation (the 'how' part). By standardizing semantics, BIAN aims to minimize the need for custom integration and promote reusability of interfaces, ultimately facilitating the seamless exchange of information between different banking systems and services.

For example, let's consider the term 'IT Service Controls'. The definition of this term can be interpreted differently by different financial organizations due to lack of standardization. In that case, what the service provider offers may not be of relevance to the service consumer. BIAN offers to solve this by providing an architecture (semantic framework) that is specifically aligned to the banking-industry. The framework follows the service integration best practices, like loose coupling, flexibility, reusability and cost efficiency.

Conclusion

In our previous chapters, we've delved into the design of effective cloud solutions by examining the available service options, guiding principles, best practices, and reference use-cases. With this solid foundation in place, we're now ready to shift our focus to the critical aspects of risk and compliance management in banking solutions.

In the next chapter, we'll explore the essential strategies and considerations for ensuring the security, integrity, and regulatory compliance of cloud-based banking solutions.

Chapter 8
Security, Risk and Compliance

Financial institutions now face a greater risk of cybercrime and fraud as a result of their increased digital presence. As more services migrate online, these organizations become more attractive targets for cybercriminals and fraudsters. Although digital platforms provide numerous advantages, such as enhanced accessibility and convenience, they also introduce new security concerns related to cybersecurity and organized financial crime. Our goal is to provide you with valuable insights, best practices, and resources to help protect your organization's sensitive data and maintain regulatory compliance.

In this chapter, we will cover:

- Importance of Security in Banking
- Types of Risk and Risk Management
- Compliance considerations, related to Cyber Security in banking

Importance of Security in Banking

Implementing strong security measures is vital for any banking system, given that these systems typically manage sensitive, personal, and confidential data. It is essential to address both unintentional (accidental) and intentional (planned) potential threats, including physical, network, application, and data threats, to safeguard this sensitive information. By prioritizing security, banking organizations can foster trust among their customers, mitigate risks, and maintain regulatory compliance.

Securing Data

Data is the backbone of any organization. Data security is crucial in today's digital age, as it protects sensitive information from unauthorized access, theft, or damage. Importance of data security can be summarized as follows:

- **Confidentiality**: Protecting sensitive information from unauthorized access, ensuring that only authorized personnel can access the data.
- **Integrity**: Ensuring that data is accurate, complete, and not tampered with during transmission, storage, or processing.
- **Availability**: Ensuring that data is accessible and usable when needed, without delays or interruptions.
- **Compliance**: Adhering to regulatory requirements, industry standards, and organizational policies to maintain data security.

Information theft is dangerous and can be used for identity fraud and many other fraudulent activities. Hence, data must be always secured. Be it at-rest, in-Use or in-Transit.

Data "At-Rest"

Data at rest is inactive data that is being stored or maintained for later use. This can include data that is being archived, backed up, or stored for historical or reference purposes. Examples of data at rest include files stored on a computer or cloud storage service, data stored in a database or data warehouse etc.

Data at rest is at risk from accidental damage, hackers, and insider threats, who can digitally access the data or physically steal the data storage media. Some of the ways to secure data at rest are:

- **Encryption**: Use encryption algorithms (e.g., Advanced Encryption Standard - AES) to scramble data, making it unreadable without the decryption key.
- **Access Control**: Implement access controls, such as user authentication and authorization, to restrict access to sensitive data.
- **Data Segregation**: Store sensitive data in separate, isolated environments or databases to prevent unauthorized access.
- **Regular Backups**: Regularly back up critical data to ensure business continuity and minimize data loss.

Data "In-Transit"

Data in transit or motion refers to the process of transmitting data over a network or the internet from one location to another. This can include data sent through various communication channels like network packets using protocols like TCP/IP, wireless connections using protocols like Wi-Fi or data stored in cloud storage services and accessed over the internet.

Data in transit is vulnerable to various security threats, including:

- **Eavesdropping**: Unauthorized access to data as it is being transmitted.
- **Tampering**: Data is altered or modified during transmission.
- **Man-in-the-middle (MitM) attacks**: An attacker intercepts and alters data between two parties.
- **Data breaches**: Unauthorized access to data stored or transmitted.
- To ensure the security of data in transit, various measures can be taken, like:
    - **Encryption**: Data is scrambled to prevent unauthorized access.
    - **Authentication**: Data is verified to ensure it comes from a trusted source.
    - **Secure protocols**: Using secure protocols like HTTPS, SSL/TLS, and IPsec.
    - **Firewalls**: Implementing firewalls to block unauthorized access.
    - **Regular updates and patches**: Keeping software and systems up to date with the latest security patches.
    - **Secure communication channels**: Using secure communication channels, such as VPNs (Virtual Private Networks).
    - **Data masking**: Hiding sensitive data to prevent unauthorized access.

Data "In-Use"

"Data in use" refers to the process of accessing, processing, and storing data within an organization's internal systems, applications, and databases. This includes data that is being actively used, processed, or stored within an organization's premises, servers, or data centers. It can include:

- **Database management**: Data is stored and managed within a database, and accessed through queries, reports, or other database operations.
- **Application processing**: Data is processed and analyzed within an application or software, such as financial transactions, customer information, or inventory management.
- **File storage**: Data is stored on local file systems, network shares, or cloud storage services, and accessed through file management tools.
- **Data analytics**: Data is analyzed and processed within an organization's data analytics tools, such as data warehouses, business intelligence platforms, or data visualization software.

Data in use is vulnerable to various security threats, including:

- **Insider threats**: Authorized personnel with access to sensitive data may misuse or compromise it.

- **Malware**: Malicious software can infect systems, steal data, or disrupt operations.
- **Unauthorized access**: Untrusted individuals may gain unauthorized access to sensitive data or systems.
- **Data breaches**: Data is stolen or compromised through unauthorized access or exploitation of vulnerabilities.

To ensure the security of data in use, we can implement various measures, like:

- **Access controls**: Implementing role-based access controls, authentication, and authorization mechanisms to restrict access to sensitive data and systems.
- **Data encryption**: Encrypting data at rest and in transit to prevent unauthorized access.
- **Data masking**: Masking sensitive data to prevent unauthorized access or exposure.
- **Regular backups**: Regularly backing up critical data to prevent data loss in the event of a disaster or system failure.
- **Monitoring and incident response**: Implementing monitoring tools and incident response plans to quickly detect and respond to security incidents.
- **Secure coding practices**: Following secure coding practices and testing to prevent vulnerabilities in software and applications.
- **Employee training**: Educating employees on data security best practices, privacy, and confidentiality.

It's essential to prioritize data security and implement robust measures to always protect data, as it can have significant consequences if compromised. In this section we looked at some of the ways to secure data. In the next section, we will understand the types of risks and how to manage them.

Types of Risks

Risks in the banking sector refer to the potential for adverse events or negative outcomes resulting from the use, operation, or implementation of information technology systems or faulty processes within a banking organization.

There are two main types (**Fig 8.1**) of risks we are covering in this chapter:

1. Financial Risks
2. Technology related risks

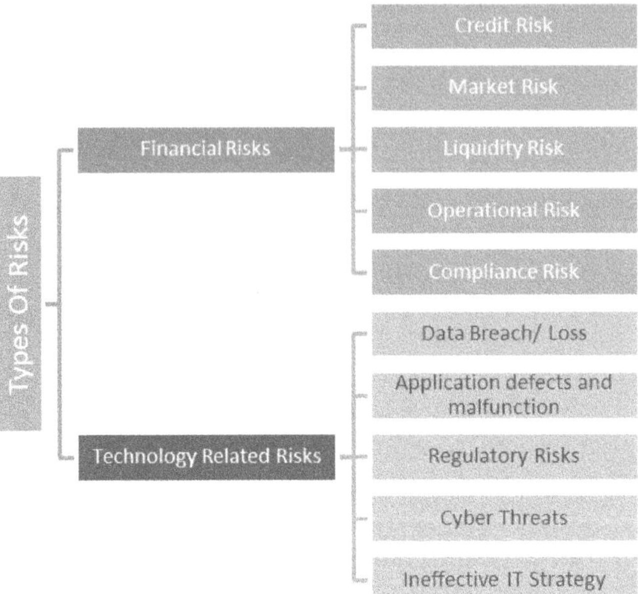

Figure 8.1: Types of Risks in Banking

Financial Risks

Risk may be defined as 'possibility of loss', which may be financial loss or loss to the image or reputation. Financial Risk is the risk that involves financial loss to firms. Financial risk generally arises due to instability and losses in the financial market caused by movements in stock prices, currencies, interest rates and more. Some of the key ones are –

- **Credit Risk** is one of the most common types of risk for banks. It is the risk of a bank lending money to a customer and not having it paid back. This can decrease the amount of assets a bank has available to meet its financial obligations.
- **Market Risk** mostly occurs from a bank's activities in capital markets. It is due to the unpredictability of equity markets, commodity prices, interest rates, and credit spreads. Banks are more exposed if they are heavily involved in investing in capital markets or sales and trading.
- **Liquidity risk** covers all risks that are associated with a bank finding itself unable to meet its commitments on time, or only being able to do so by recourse to emergency borrowing.
- **Operational Risk** arises out of operational failures such as mismanagement or technical failures. Operational risk can be classified into Fraud Risk and Model Risk. Fraud risk arises due to the lack of controls and Model risk arises

due to incorrect model application.

- **Compliance Risk** is the risk to earnings or capital arising from violations of, or non-conformance with, laws, rules, regulations, prescribed practices, or ethical standards. Compliance risk also arises in situations where the laws or rules governing certain bank products or activities of the bank's clients may be ambiguous or untested. Compliance risk exposes the institution to fines, civil money penalties, payment of damages, and the voiding of contracts. Compliance risk can lead to a diminished reputation.

Technology Related Risks

Technology risk arises from the use of computer systems in the day-to-day conduct of the bank's operations, reconciliation of books of accounts, and storage and retrieval of information and reports. The risk can occur due to the choice of faulty or unsuitable technology and adoption of untried or obsolete technology. Major risk arises from breaches of security for access to the computer system, tampering with the system, and unauthorized use of it. Some technology related risks are:

- **Software Defect / Application Malfunction**: Many banks got into the headlines because of software malfunctions that caused serious inconveniences to their customers. A phenomenally simple software error can affect the life of millions of people in the most direct and negative way. For e.g. A software bug that occurred in the system of a big network provider in 2021 knocked banks, airlines, and other companies all over the world offline during peak business hours in Asia, only some days after another major web services company crushed and world's top websites went offline due to a software bug that triggered when a single customer changed a setting. Banking services of Westpac, the Commonwealth Bank, ANZ, St George, and other financial institutions went all down not because of a cyber-attack but because of a glitch which disrupted the service that protects them against DoS (denial-of-service attacks).

- **Regulatory Risks**: Banks are one of the most heavily regulated business sectors, with stiff regulatory compliance obligations and scrutiny from regulators. Compliance failures can result in huge penalties, reputational damage, bad publicity, and even lawsuits. It's vital for banks to conduct regular compliance risk assessments to identify, evaluate and mitigate emerging risks. Regulatory risks owing to technology may arise from a bank's failure to comply with laws, regulations, and industry standards related to that sector. This includes risks associated with anti-money laundering (AML), know-your-customer (KYC) requirements, data privacy, consumer protection, financial stability, and other areas. Some examples of regulatory risk are:

- o Data privacy and cybersecurity breaches. The ultimate purpose of data privacy is to uphold public expectations, so banks have a duty of care when handling personally identifiable information (PII). The absence of robust cybersecurity procedures, effective policies, or internal controls can all expose banks to risks, ranging from potential data breaches and financial fraud to the endangerment of confidential client information.
  - o Anti-Money laundering (AML) violations. Banks found guilty of AML violations can face significant legal and regulatory consequences, including fines and reputational damage. The 2019 statistics on penalties levied against banks revealed that more than 60 percent of fines were the result of non-compliance with AML regulations. AML compliance refers to processes, regulations, technological solutions, and other initiatives that combat money laundering efforts, keeping illegitimate funds from entering legitimate financial flows.
  - o Customer due diligence (CDD) failures. A bank's failure to identify and authenticate its customers' identities adequately, and to understand those customers' business activities, financial transactions, and risk exposure, are referred to as CDD failures, which can greatly affect the bank's risk profile. Inaccurate client identification and verification, poor record-keeping, and inadequate customer transaction monitoring are the most common causes of CDD failures.
  - o Consumer protection violations. Banks should deal fairly and honestly with consumers at all stages of their relationship to avoid consumer compliance risks and causing consumer harm, whether through deceptive practices, unfair fees, or other forms of mistreatment. Consumers should receive up-to-date information from financial services companies about new products and services; that information must be easily accessible, simple to understand, and not in any way deceptive. Banks that are found to be violating consumer protection laws can suffer damage to their reputation, which might result in a loss of clients and reputation.
- **Cyber Threats** are often caused by malicious software, such as viruses, ransomware, and malware. The primary goals of cyber attackers and hackers are to steal sensitive information or disrupt normal operations. This can include making banking applications unavailable or damaging a bank's reputation. Some examples of the cyber-attacks which resulted in data breaches and loss of reputation are as follows:
  - o **Yahoo – 3 billion:** Yahoo disclosed that a breach in August 2013 by a group of hackers had compromised 1 billion accounts. The breach was first reported by Yahoo on December 14, 2016, and forced all affected users to change passwords, and to reenter any unencrypted security questions and answers to make them encrypted in the

future.

- o **Verifications.io - 763 million**: In February 2019, email address validation service verifications.io exposed 763 million unique email addresses in a MongoDB instance that was left publicly facing with no password. Many records also included names, phone numbers, IP addresses, dates of birth and genders.
- o **Marriott/Starwood - 500 million**: In November 2018, Marriott International announced that hackers had stolen data about approximately 500 million Starwood hotel customers. The attackers had gained unauthorized access to the Starwood system back in 2014 and remained in the system after Marriott acquired Starwood in 2016. However, the discovery was not made until 2018.

- **Ineffective IT Strategy**: Companies often must decide on the right IT strategy and the pace at which they want to adapt the new technology and the return on investment. They may choose to watch new technologies evolve instead of embracing them. Companies must balance the risk of adopting new technology and waiting for things to settle down or ignoring the technology outright. There may also be a misalignment between business and IT strategies. This could lead to unnecessary investments and unfulfilled expectations.

Risk Management

Risk management is the process of identifying, assessing, and mitigating potential risks that could negatively impact an organization's objectives, assets, or reputation. It involves a proactive approach to managing uncertainty to minimize the likelihood and impact of adverse events.

Risk Management Steps

Risk management provides different approaches that can be used to deal with the risks and reward tradeoffs of a potential opportunity. The risk management process typically involves the following steps:

Figure 8.2: Risk Management Steps

Step 1: Risk Identification

The first step is to identify the potential risks that may occur. These may be internal threats that arise from within a company or from outside forces. To identify risks, a security assessment needs to be done on the design by a Security Architect. Examples of risks: System being hacked due to ineffective authentication mechanism, data loss due to system crash, system being unavailable due to a natural disaster in a location (like floods)

Step 2: Identify Likeliness of Occurrence

Once the Risks are listed, next step is to identify the likeliness of the risk to occur. The question to be asked is – what the odds for the situation are to occur. The system being hacked or data loss due to a system crash are more likely to occur. A situation like a flood occurring depends on the geography and could be very rare in some areas.

Step 3: Estimate Impact

Most often, the goal of a risk analysis is to better understand how risk will financially impact a company. The Impact my be categorized as High, Medium., or low. For example, the impact of the situation where a flood occurs would be very-high, because that would render the system to be down for a long duration, while the impact of a critical resource quitting their job is low, as you can very likely find a replacement for that person.

Every risk that has been identified can be assigned a risk value, which is the probability of an event happening multiplied by the impact caused of the event. Risk Value is usually calculated by a heat-map, which is a powerful visualization tool. It is a graph between the risk-occurrence likely hood vs the impact. As part of the risk management strategy, organizations should define categorization of each the criteria.

Step 4: Build Analysis Model(s)

The inputs from above are often fed into an analysis model. The analysis model will take all available pieces of data and information, and the model will attempt to yield different outcomes, probabilities, and financial projections of what may occur. In more advanced situations, scenario analysis or simulations can determine an average outcome value that can be used to quantify the average instance of an event occurring.

Step 5: Analyze Results

With the model run and the data available to be reviewed, the next step is to analyze the results. Management often takes the information and determines the best course of action by comparing the likelihood of risk, projected financial impact, and model simulations. Management may also request different scenarios run for different risks based on different variables or inputs.

The outcome of the risk analysis could be a strategic plan to mitigate the identified risk. This plan may involve accepting the risk and taking no further action, which is often referred to as risk acceptance. In cases where risk acceptance is chosen, a company may decide that it is more financially beneficial to continue as usual and address any potential issues that arise after the fact. Alternatively, management may opt to reduce or eliminate the risk altogether by implementing measures to mitigate its impact.

Types of Risk Analysis

As depicted in Fig 8.3 and explained in proceeding sections:

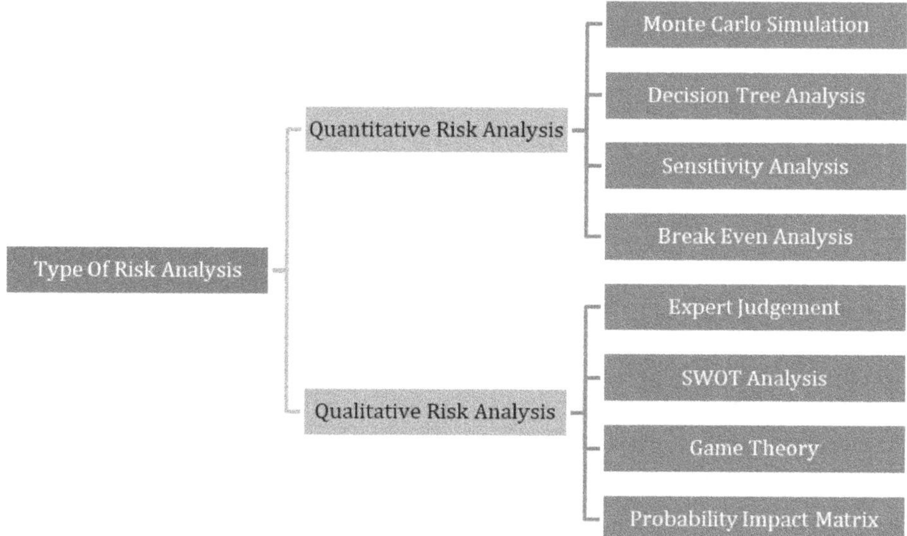

Figure 8.3: Types of Risk Analysis

- **Quantitative Risk Analysis**: In this the risk model is built using simulation or deterministic statistics to assign numerical values to risk. Inputs that are mostly assumptions and random variables are fed into a risk model. For any given range of input, the model generates a range of output or outcome. The model's output is analyzed using graphs, scenario analysis, and/or sensitivity analysis by risk managers to make decisions to mitigate and deal with the risks. For e.g. A Monte Carlo simulation can be used to generate a range of possible outcomes of a decision made or action taken. Other examples are decision trees and break-even analysis.

- **Qualitative Risk Analysis**: is an analytical method that does not identify and evaluate risks with numerical and quantitative ratings. Qualitative analysis involves a written definition of the uncertainties, an evaluation of the extent of the impact (if the risk ensues), and countermeasure plans in the case of a negative event occurring. Examples of qualitative risk tools include SWOT analysis, cause and effect diagrams, decision matrix, game theory, etc.

Step 6: Implement Solutions

After analyzing and understanding the risk, the next step is to develop and implement a plan to mitigate it. This involves putting in place suitable controls and preventive measures to minimize or eliminate the risk. For instance, to address the risk of disaster caused by floods, a company might develop a Disaster Recovery (DR) strategy that includes building a secondary site where critical systems can be operated in the event the primary site becomes unavailable. Similarly, to mitigate the risk of data loss due to system crashes, a company could implement a regular backup process, allowing them to restore the system and data when needed.

In the next section, we understood the steps for managing the risks. In the next section, we will look at the best practices to manage risks – both for technology related risks and in general.

Risk Management – Best Practices

We have looked at the types of risks, risk management and the risk analysis in the last section. In this section, we will discuss some of the best practices for effective risk management programs.

Cyber Security – Best Practices

Some of the cybersecurity best practices which help address the Technology related risks for banking applications.

- Performing Regular VA+PT to Stay Compliant with Regulations Conducting Regular Vulnerability Assessments and Penetration Testing can quickly help financial companies and banks detect and remediate vulnerabilities that could lead to data breaches. Financial services can also use these regular tests to strengthen their security posture and meet the stringent cyber resilience requirements of most regulations.

- Implement a Zero-Trust Policy Until proven differently, a zero-trust design considers all network activity as malicious. This framework promotes more secure privileged access management, making it harder for threat actors to gain access to critical information. Have an Incident Response Plan Having a properly framed Cybersecurity Incident Response Plan in advance can guide your IT and cybersecurity experts on how to respond to a significant security incident, such as a data breach, data leak, ransomware attack, or loss of critical data.
- Manage Third Party-Risks In order to make the systems ready for regulation compliance, it is essential to manage the third-party risks. It will secure your entire third-party vendor network by certifying cybersecurity preparedness with security ratings and evaluating compliance with security assessments. Advanced TPRM (Third Party Risk Management) solutions can additionally map security assessment responses to vendor-specific mandated rules to detect flaws that prohibit compliance.
- Encrypt Valuable Data leaks not only hasten data breaches but also disclose sensitive information that may be in violation of regulations. That is why encrypting the data has become critical. Encryption can address the risks associated with exposures both inside and across the vendor network, help avoid regulatory infractions and the penalties that come with them if they go unnoticed.
- Combating Local Malicious Software and Phishing – Phishing technique is used by fraudsters to acquire user credentials (like username, password) and other sensitive information through social engineering by masquerading as a legitimate website, message or other communication. Credentials stolen are generally captured and sent to a command control service then used or resold for later use by criminals. To combat the same, solutions should use solutions like Enhanced Multi factor Authentication and VeriSign Secure Site Pro with Extended Validation SSL Certificates.

Other Best Practices

These were the best practices to manage the technology-related risks. Let's also understand some of the recommendations for managing the risks in general for financial organizations.

Establish the risk Governance framework

Establishing a risk governance framework enables a more collaborative approach to risk management, involving a broader range of stakeholders within the bank, including risk and compliance teams, as well as other departments. This shared responsibility helps to ensure that all stakeholders understand the bank's risk profile and the importance of managing those risks effectively.

Once risks are identified, they should be assigned to the relevant departments, where team leaders will develop and implement tailored risk management strategies. This decentralized approach ensures that each department is equipped to manage its own risks, fostering a culture of risk awareness and responsibility across the entire institution.

Prioritize identity verification

Securing sensitive information by limiting access to authorized individuals is a critical objective. The Know Your Customer (KYC) process helps prevent identity fraud and unauthorized activities, ensuring that individuals are who they claim to be. The Know Your Business (KYB) process is equally important, as it verifies the legitimacy of a business and identifies its true ownership structure, thereby preventing the use of shell companies for illicit activities. The Know Your Employee (KYE) process is also vital, as it ensures that bank employees act with integrity and do not misuse their privileged access to information, which could compromise the bank's security and lead to potential risks.

Automating Risk Management

Take help of technology to automate the tasks related to the risk management. This helps alert about the suspicious activities at the nascent stage and allows a bank's risk management team to better prioritize which alerts warrant a manual investigation or serious action.

Continually assess, analyze, and act on risk metrics

In the dynamic world of banking, risk management is an ongoing process that requires constant adaptation. As a bank's staff, clientele, and technology evolve, so do the potential risks and threats. To stay ahead, banks must regularly review and update their risk management strategies to ensure they remain effective and relevant.

This involves continuously assessing their current controls and mitigation plans to identify areas for improvement. Banks must also anticipate potential future risks and develop systems that can adapt to manage them effectively.

It's crucial to create and regularly update risk management plans based on thorough analysis and implement robust governance structures to ensure all employees are aware of their roles and responsibilities in managing risks. By doing so, banks can maintain a strong foundation for risk management and protect their operations and customers.

In this section, we looked at the best practices to manage risks. In the next section, we will understand the impact of non-compliance and the measures which businesses need to keep in mind to ensure the IT systems are compliant.

Compliance Considerations related to Cyber Security in Banking

Non-Compliance involves neglecting the established security protocols which leaves the organizations vulnerable to malicious actors. There are a host of measures that businesses need to consider when ensuring their IT systems are compliant. These include keeping software up to date such as operating systems, maintaining the best practice security and firewall measures, meeting the requirements of industry specific measures such as the Payment Card Industry Data Security Standard (PCI DSS) or the General Data Protection Regulation (GDPR), and accounting for local and regional government regulations.

Businesses that don't comply with regulations are at serious risk. They could face security breaches, loss of productivity, and reputational damage. Non-compliance might also lead to financial penalties, loss of clientele, disruptions in operations, and even regional lockouts. Cyber criminals use sophisticated techniques and work around the clock looking for vulnerabilities in systems across organizations around the globe, and such is the risk in the modern digitalized world that an attempted cyber-attack is increasingly becoming a matter of "when", not "if", for organizations that fail to keep their IT systems updated and compliant.

Not only can cyber-attacks result in massive financial cost to a business in terms of fines from regulatory bodies, (such as a £20m fine in the case of British Airways failing to protect the personal details of more than 400,000 of its customers), but it can also be detrimental in a much wider sense depending on the industry. For example, for organizations that are part of extensive supply chains or providing systems to other businesses, a single cyber-attack can prove disastrous across organizations that rely on partners and third-party software.

Another key example of an industry-specific implication was the WannaCry cyber-attack on the NHS in 2017, where a major ransomware attack led to 6,900 critical appointments being cancelled, leading to a direct impact on livelihoods in the UK. In almost all cases, major incidents such as these could have been avoided with updated and compliant systems in place.

As we see in the examples above, the consequences of non-compliance can be fatal. Some of them being:

Regulatory Fines/ Penalties

Regulators impose huge fines on non-compliant companies to ensure the safety and security of the citizens. GDPR fines alone can cost 4% of revenue. There are also investigational costs, legal fees, breach fixes, and payouts to affected customers. Depending on the violation, fines can really stack up.

Reputational Risk

Firms with strong positive reputations attract more customers. In an economy where 70% to 80% of market value comes from hard-to-assess intangible assets such as brand equity, intellectual capital, and goodwill, organizations are especially vulnerable to anything that damages their reputations.

Non-compliance can quickly cause customers to lose trust and loyalty. People will look for alternative solutions and choose those alternative organizations that take security and compliance more seriously.

Legal Liability Risk

Legal liability risks include both the civil and criminal liabilities. For major compliance failures, individuals can land behind bars for months or years and/or organizations shutdown. For example, a HIPAA violation where the organization knowingly obtained or disclosed personal health information can lead to imprisonment of up to one year.

Disrupted business activities

Missing out on crucial cybersecurity strategies and improper implementation of compliance frameworks puts the organization behind its competitors. Data breaches cause downtime, sinking productivity and profits. For example, in major violations, PCI DSS non-compliance can lead to businesses losing their license to process credit cards.

Conclusion

In conclusion, the banking sector is a complex and dynamic environment that is constantly evolving in response to technological advancements, changing regulatory requirements, and shifting customer expectations. As a result, banks must prioritize security, risk, and compliance to maintain the trust of their customers, regulators, and stakeholders.

Effective security, risk, and compliance management requires a proactive and adaptive approach that incorporates robust governance structures, robust risk assessments, and continuous monitoring and improvement. In this chapter, we learned about the importance of securing data, types of risks, how to manage risks and the compliance considerations. We also looked at the risk analysis techniques and best practices to be adopted to mitigate them.

In the next chapter, we will peek into the future and look at the how the recent advancements in technology are impacting the IT landscape in Banking industry.

References

https://www.upguard.com/blog/data-breach

https://www.validata-software.com/blog-mobi/item/447-banks-busted-by-a-software-glitch-during-2021

https://reciprocity.com/resources/what-is-a-compliance-risk-assessment/

https://www.unit21.ai/blog/risk-management-in-banking

https://www.investopedia.com/

Chapter 9
Peek into the future

As we venture into the realm of "Peek into the Future" for banking IT, this chapter will provide a thoughtful and informative introduction to the evolving trends that will shape the future. As we witnessed in the previous chapters, banking IT is currently characterized by:

- **Digitalization**: The widespread adoption of digital channels has become essential for banks to stay competitive. Online and mobile banking platforms, as well as social media and messaging apps, have become the norm.
- **Cloud Computing**: Cloud-based solutions have enabled banks to reduce infrastructure costs, increase scalability, and improve disaster recovery capabilities.
- **Artificial Intelligence (AI) and Machine Learning (ML)**: AI and ML are being leveraged to enhance customer service, automate processes, and improve risk management.
- **Cybersecurity**: The rise of digital banking has introduced new cybersecurity threats, making it essential for banks to invest in robust security measures to protect customer data.
- **Open Banking**: The increasing adoption of open APIs has enabled banks to share data and services with third-party providers, fostering innovation and competition.

As we embark on this journey to peek into the future of banking IT, we'll explore several innovative advancements which are predicted to revolutionize the sector. We will be examining their potential impact on the industry and the opportunities they present. Get ready to be inspired by the exciting possibilities that await us on this path forward!

In this chapter, we will cover some of the technology trends impacting the banking industry:

- Integration of AI, GenAi and ML in Financial solutions

- Hyper Personalization
- Focus on enhanced Cyber Security
- Quantum Computing Advancements
- Block Chain and Cryptocurrencies

Deeper Integration of AI / ML in Financial Applications

Artificial Intelligence (AI), is transforming industries with its recent breakthroughs, offering exciting possibilities alongside challenges that demand attention. AI has already burst into the mainstream and organizations are experimenting with actual use cases to harness its true power.

The financial services industry utilizes AI in large-scale tasks and data analysis already. Firms are discovering numerous benefits associated with AI adoption. According to a recent survey by Gartner, the top benefits of artificial intelligence (AI) implementation in 2023 are improved productivity and efficiency, which are experienced by 75% of respondents, enhanced customer experience, which is reported by 60% of respondents, and reduced costs, which is a benefit enjoyed by 54% of respondents.

There is bound to be deeper integration of AI in the banking applications to attain improved problem-solving, image recognition, enhanced user experience, increased automation to reduce cost and bridge skill gaps. AI integration has the potential to lead to creative solutions across the financial sector.

Some use cases which are already implemented and being explored using AI/ ML algorithms and Data science capabilities are:

- **Better Personalization experiences**: AI-powered algorithms can help personalize the products and services like targeted offers, wealth management advice, and risk assessments.
- **Fraud detection and prevention**: Advanced AI systems can help prevent cyberattacks and financial crimes, protecting both the financial institutes and consumers.
- **Increased Automation and assisted decision-making**: AI can help streamline and automate the operational processes including customer service, loan disbursements, account handling, bill processing etc. which would result in improved efficiency and scalability.
- **Trading Algorithms:** One of the common problems in trading is getting market analysis too late to take advantage of opportunities. AI finance tools can outperform human trades and bring faster and better decisions

on trading. The comprehensive analysis of different market aspects and factors with the help of AI, allows banks to achieve new heights in trading algorithms.

- **Risk Management:** Artificial intelligence in financial services makes a huge difference in investment management and risk analysis. AI can accurately estimate the client's creditworthiness and answer the crucial question: is this person reliable? The AI-based system can analyze the risks by considering transaction and credit history, income growth, market conditions, etc.
- **Regulations and Compliance**: AI driven algorithms can take into account all the regulations, detect deviations, analyze data and follows the rules accurately.

Implementation of Generative AI in Real Life applications

While AI has proven beneficial to finance businesses in diverse ways, the finance industry has embraced Generative AI and is extensively harnessing its power. While traditional AI/ML is focused on making predictions or classifications based on existing data, generative AI creates novel content by analyzing patterns in existing data. This versatile technology can generate content in a wide range of modalities, including text, images, code, and music, making it ideal for a range of use cases. Its potential to enhance accuracy and efficiency has made it increasingly popular in the finance and banking industries.

Generative Artificial Intelligence (Gen AI) is a cutting-edge technology built on large language models that can learn from vast amounts of data and produce responses to user queries. This innovative technology is revolutionizing the digital landscape, ushering in a new era of digital innovation. Although still in its early stages of adoption, Gen AI has the capability to analyze massive datasets, uncovering hidden patterns and trends, and leveraging this insight to make informed decisions.

The application of generative AI in finance holds the potential to redefine traditional approaches by generating realistic and informative financial scenarios, enhancing portfolio optimization strategies, enabling sophisticated risk simulations and fraud detection and more.

Along with all the areas where AI is already bringing in differentiation, some more potential use cases where Gen AI capabilities are being leveraged by the industry are:

- **Chatbots and virtual assistants**: Generative AI plays a crucial role in empowering virtual agents to generate contextually relevant and human-like responses, creating seamless and dynamic conversations. By analyzing vast data, generative AI enables virtual agents to offer personalized, tailored, and accurate responses, improving overall customer satisfaction.

- **Financial document search and synthesis**: Within banking and other financial services, the efficient search and synthesis of crucial financial documents are paramount for informed decision-making. Generative AI aids analysts in researching and summarizing economic data, credit memos, underwriting documents, and regulatory filings. Generative AI fundamentally transforms how financial documents are managed, presenting a dynamic and efficient methodology for banking and financial sector professionals.
- **Financial product innovation and design**: Leveraging advanced algorithms, financial institutions employ generative design to create innovative products by exploring many possibilities and optimizing for specific criteria. The automation of product ideation and prototyping processes streamlines development cycles, enabling rapid design iterations. Furthermore, generative in customer-centric approaches, sentiment analysis tools analyze feedback, social media posts, and reviews, providing valuable insights for improving banking services and products.
- **Marketing and lead generation**: In the fiercely competitive financial landscape, targeted marketing is crucial for attracting new customers. Generative AI becomes a valuable ally in this process, contributing to the creation of personalized marketing materials tailored to specific customer segments.
- **Advanced Transaction Prediction**: Financial institutions are delving into the use of generative models for predicting customer transactions and suggesting relevant products or features.
- **Enhanced Investment Analysis**: Investment firms are beginning to use Generative AI for producing detailed reports on companies, merging textual and structured data for more comprehensive insights.
- **Code generation and conversion**: By automating coding processes, institutions can save time, reduce errors and improve the efficiency of their software development operations. This enables faster development of applications and enhances the overall development lifecycle efficiency by providing features like code generation, optimization, refactoring, migration, documentation and generation of regression and unit test cases. Example: Github copilot enables NLP to understand simple English like statements in the form of requirements or code comments to generate code in popular languages like python. This can range from auto completion of code to generating functions or blocks of code.

The future of Generative AI in the financial sector is poised to transform the industry's landscape, with a focus on redefining the way humans and computers interact and processing information more efficiently. The next few years will be pivotal for financial institutions, as they move beyond pilot projects and scale up the adoption of GenAI-powered solutions, enabling widespread implementation of use cases that drive innovation and growth.

Hyper-Personalization in Banking

Hyper-personalization in banking refers to the use of advanced technologies to provide highly tailored financial products and services to individual customers. This approach aims to create a unique and personalized experience for each customer, considering their individual needs, preferences, behaviors, and financial situations.

Hyper-personalization in banking involves using large amounts of customer data, including:

- **Transactional data**: Information about customer transactions, such as spending habits, payment patterns, and account activity.
- **Behavioral data**: Insights into customer behavior, such as login patterns, search queries, and browsing history.
- **Demographic data**: Information about customer demographics, such as age, location, and occupation.
- **Psychographic data**: Insights into customer preferences, values, and attitudes.

By combining and analyzing these data sources, banks can create highly detailed customer profiles, enabling them to:

- **Offer tailored financial products**: Banks can create customized financial products, such as credit cards, loans, and investment portfolios, that are tailored to individual customers' needs and risk tolerance.
- **Provide personalized services**: Banks can offer personalized services, such as financial advice, investment guidance, and customer support, that are tailored to individual customers' needs and preferences.
- **Enhance customer engagement**: Banks can use hyper-personalization to engage customers more effectively, by sending targeted offers, promotions, and communications that are relevant to their individual needs and interests.
- **Improve customer retention**: By providing a highly personalized experience, banks can increase customer satisfaction and loyalty, reducing the likelihood of customers switching to competitor banks.

Some examples of hyper-personalization in banking include:

- **Customized credit card offers**: A bank may offer a customer a credit card with a specific interest rate, rewards program, and credit limit based on their individual credit score, spending habits, and financial situation.
- **Personalized investment portfolios**: A bank may create a customized investment portfolio for a customer based on their risk tolerance, investment

goals, and financial situation.

- **Targeted marketing campaigns**: A bank may use hyper-personalization to create targeted marketing campaigns that are tailored to individual customers' interests, behaviors, and preferences.
- **AI-powered financial advisors**: A bank may use AI-powered financial advisors that can provide personalized financial advice and guidance to individual customers based on their unique financial situation and goals.

Overall, hyper-personalization in banking aims to create a more personalized and engaging experience for customers, increasing customer satisfaction, loyalty, and retention, while also driving revenue growth and profitability for the bank.

Focus on Enhanced Cybersecurity

As technology advances, so do the threats to cybersecurity. To stay ahead, it's crucial to adopt cutting-edge solutions like zero-trust architectures, blockchain-based security protocols, and AI-driven threat detection. Proactive measures are necessary to safeguard digital assets, as cyberattacks are becoming increasingly sophisticated.

According to the 2024 CrowdStrike global threat report, electronic crime (eCrime) remains the most prevalent threat, and data-theft extortion continues to rise. In 2023, there was a significant 76% increase in victims listed on eCrime dedicated leak sites compared to 2022. As companies rely more on technology, they inadvertently create more opportunities for sophisticated cyberattacks.

Financial institutions cannot afford to ignore data security or neglect advanced technological solutions in today's digital age. Therefore, it's essential to develop effective strategies to defend against cyberattacks and mitigate the risks associated with excessive technology and data use. Prioritizing cybersecurity preparedness, implementing robust security measures, and adopting proactive approaches across the sector is the only way forward.

Cybersecurity spending is expected to increase over the next two to three years, with regional banks (Tier 2) likely to experience the greatest growth. This anticipated growth may be driven by Tier 2 banks nearing the Tier 1 capital threshold and anticipating increased regulatory scrutiny.

Achieving enhanced cyber security in banking requires a multi-layered approach that involves implementing robust security measures, staying up to date with the latest threats, and fostering a culture of security awareness within the organization. Here are some steps to help achieve enhanced cyber security in banking by building IT solutions to:

- Implement a robust security framework
- Protect against external threats
- Protect against internal threats
- Stay up to date with the latest threats
- Foster a culture of security awareness
- Implement a secure architecture
- Monitor and analyze security logs
- Conduct regular security testing
- Implement a incident response plan
- Collaborate with other financial institutions and law enforcement agencies

By following these steps, financial institutions can significantly enhance their cyber security posture and reduce the risk of security breaches.

Quantum Computing Advancements

A recent McKinsey study highlights the finance sector's potential to greatly benefit from quantum computing. Banks and financial institutions already rely on intricate calculations to analyze and predict market trends, but quantum computers can solve even more complex problems, faster and more accurately than traditional computers.

Within the financial sector, quantum computers can enable the analysis of vast amounts of stock market data, previously too numerous and random to process. Additionally, in loan and portfolio calculations, quantum computers promise enhanced precision in credit assessments, enabling more informed lending decisions. Moreover, quantum computers can be used to detect fraud with increased accuracy, resulting in significant cost savings for banks.

The most significant applications of quantum computing are in corporate banking, where high-stakes transactions and complex use cases in areas such as trade finance drive the need for advanced risk management and analysis. The risk management unit, in particular, is a complex and critical area, as it involves identifying, mitigating, and reporting risks across various business units. With quantum computing, regulatory reporting associated with risk will likely undergo a significant transformation. Quantum machine learning can enable decision makers to consider a broader range of variables and assets when simulating risks, reducing the cost of risk and facilitating larger, high-margin deals.

Quantum computing has immense potential to bring significant value to the finance sector, with benefits including real-time automated decision making and support activities such as holistic simulations of liquidity and risk assessments as part of large-scale, high-margin deals.

Sustainable Technology Solutions

Sustainable technology solutions for banking refer to the implementation of environmentally friendly, socially responsible, and economically viable practices and technologies that minimize the industry's ecological footprint and promote a positive impact on society. Here are some examples of sustainable technology solutions for banking:

- **Cloud Computing**: Migrating to cloud computing can significantly reduce energy consumption and carbon emissions associated with data center operations. Cloud providers can also offer sustainable infrastructure options, such as renewable energy-powered data centers.
- **Digital Payments**: Digital payments reduce the need for physical cash and can help reduce waste, energy consumption, and carbon emissions associated with cash handling and processing.
- **Blockchain Technology**: Blockchain technology can enable secure, transparent, and efficient transactions, reducing the need for intermediaries and minimizing the risk of fraud. This can lead to cost savings, increased security, and reduced energy consumption.
- **Green Banking Platforms**: Banks can develop green banking platforms that offer sustainable investment options, such as green bonds, and provide customers with information on the environmental impact of their financial decisions.
- **Paperless Banking**: Implementing paperless banking practices can reduce paper waste, energy consumption, and carbon emissions associated with printing and processing paper documents.
- **Energy-Efficient Data Centers**: Banks can invest in energy-efficient data centers that use renewable energy sources, such as solar or wind power, to reduce their carbon footprint.
- **Sustainable Supply Chain Management**: Banks can implement sustainable supply chain management practices, such as sourcing materials and services from environmentally responsible suppliers, to minimize their ecological impact.
- **Online Banking**: Online banking can reduce the need for physical branches, reducing energy consumption, water usage, and waste generation associated with building and maintaining physical infrastructure.
- **Artificial Intelligence (AI) and Machine Learning (ML)**: AI and ML can help banks optimize their operations, reduce waste, and improve customer experience while minimizing their environmental impact.
- Cryptocurrencies: Cryptocurrencies, such as Bitcoin, can provide a secure, decentralized, and transparent way to conduct transactions, reducing the need for intermediaries and minimizing the risk of fraud.
- **Sustainable Investment Products**: Banks can offer sustainable investment

products, such as socially responsible investment (SRI) funds, that align with customers' values and promote environmentally friendly and socially responsible practices.

- **Environmental Impact Assessments**: Banks can conduct environmental impact assessments to identify and mitigate the environmental effects of their operations, products, and services.
- **Sustainable Infrastructure**: Banks can invest in sustainable infrastructure, such as green buildings, renewable energy projects, and sustainable transportation systems, to support their customers' sustainable lifestyles.
- **Customer Education and Engagement**: Banks can educate and engage their customers on sustainable banking practices, such as using digital payments, reducing paper usage, and making sustainable investment decisions.
- **Partnerships and Collaborations**: Banks can partner with organizations, such as environmental NGOs, to promote sustainable banking practices, share best practices, and support environmentally friendly projects and initiatives.

By implementing these sustainable technology solutions, banks can reduce their environmental impact, promote social responsibility, and contribute to a more sustainable future.

We will discuss in detail the Sustainable Technology Solution and it's best practices in Chapter 10 – "Sustainable Cloud Technology Solutions".

Blockchain and Cryptocurrencies

Blockchain and cryptocurrencies are poised to have a significant impact on the future of banking IT. Blockchain technology provides a secure, decentralized ledger that can be used for transactions without the need for intermediaries such as banks. Cryptocurrencies like Bitcoin have gained popularity as an alternative to traditional currencies, and their value has skyrocketed in recent years.

The forecast suggests that blockchain and cryptocurrencies will continue to expand, with an increasing number of businesses and individuals utilizing digital currencies for transactions. Blockchain technology has the potential to simplify banking and lending processes, reducing the risk of counterparty default and decreasing the time it takes to issue and settle transactions. This technology also enables secured storage and verification of documentation, including Know Your Customer (KYC) and Anti-Money Laundering (AML) data. It is likely that major banks will eventually adopt blockchain technology and collaborate with each other to leverage its benefits. Here are some potential effects of Blockchain technology on IT solutions in Banking:

- **Increased security**: Blockchain technology is known for its secure and transparent nature, which can help reduce the risk of cyber-attacks and data breaches in the banking sector. As a result, banks may adopt blockchain-based solutions to improve the security of their systems and protect customer data.
- **Decentralized architecture**: Blockchain technology allows for decentralized transactions, which can reduce the need for intermediaries and increase efficiency. Banks may adopt decentralized architecture to reduce costs and improve customer experience.
- **Faster transactions**: Blockchain technology enables faster and more efficient transactions, which can reduce the time it takes for funds to clear and settle. This can be particularly beneficial for cross-border transactions.
- **New business models**: Cryptocurrencies and blockchain technology can enable new business models, such as peer-to-peer lending, decentralized finance (DeFi), and tokenized assets. Banks may need to adapt to these new models and find ways to integrate them into their existing operations.
- **Increased transparency**: Blockchain technology provides a transparent and tamper-proof record of transactions, which can help improve accountability and trust in the banking system.
- **Improved customer experience**: Blockchain technology can enable faster and more secure transactions, which can improve the overall customer experience and increase customer satisfaction.
- **Reduced costs**: Blockchain technology can reduce the need for intermediaries and increase efficiency, which can lead to cost savings for banks and customers.
- **New revenue streams**: Blockchain technology can enable new revenue streams for banks, such as providing blockchain-based services to other industries, such as supply chain management and identity verification.
- **Regulatory uncertainty**: The regulatory landscape around blockchain and cryptocurrencies is still evolving, which can create uncertainty and challenges for banks as they navigate this new technology.

To prepare for the impact of blockchain and cryptocurrencies, banks may need to:

- Develop a deep understanding of blockchain technology and its applications in the banking sector.
- Invest in blockchain development and talent acquisition.
- Develop strategies for integrating blockchain technology into existing operations.
- Focus on regulatory compliance and risk management.
- Develop new business models and revenue streams.
- Improve customer experience and engagement.
- Stay up to date with industry trends and developments.

Overall, the impact of blockchain and cryptocurrencies on the future of banking IT will be significant, and the banks which are prepared to adapt to these changes will be better positioned to succeed in the long term.

Conclusion

To conclude, the trends outlined above will impact the financial services sector over the coming years. The future of the finance industry is exciting and full of opportunities, but it's also rapidly changing. Financial institutions would have to take a strategic and balanced approach to embrace new technologies, comply with changing regulations, and adapt to changing consumer preferences. The rise of fintech startups and other new players is also disrupting the industry, but it is also creating new opportunities for innovation and growth. As we look to the future, it's important to keep an eye on emerging trends and predictions to ensure that the organization stays competitive and relevant in the ever-changing finance industry.

Chapter 10
Sustainable Cloud Technology Solutions

In previous chapters, we have discussed how to leverage cloud technologies to deliver efficient banking IT solutions. As we continue to increase our dependency on technology to solve our problems, it is important for us to understand the associated impacts on the environment and further try to reduce any adverse impacts.

In this chapter we will see how to build sustainable cloud-based technology solutions by discussing on the following topics

- Sustainability and its relevance
- Understanding Green IT
- Sustainable Cloud Computing
- Best Practices for Green Cloud Computing

Sustainability and its relevance

As we increase our dependency on technology to solve our everyday problems, there is an ever-growing demand for more powerful systems, with increased hardware and computing power to support these systems. Over the past few decades, this has resulted in adverse effects to our environment during production of the equipment, their use and also as part of disposing end-of-life equipment.

We now are better informed about these impacts, and this has resulted in growing concerns about increasing carbon footprint and Greenhouse Gas Emissions that are resulting in adverse impact to our environment. The concept of sustainability helps strike a balance and lately there has been growing focus in this area to help minimize the negative long-term environmental impacts.

Sustainability is about making sure we use resources, like energy and materials, in a way that we don't run out of them or harm the environment. It means thinking about the needs of people in the present and in the future, and balancing economic, social, and environmental concerns. By being sustainable, we can save money, be more efficient, and be kinder to the planet.

Sustainability is a critical concept in modern technology design and implementation, encompassing the principles and practices that promote long-term ecological balance in harmony with the use of Information Technology. Green IT is considered a big step towards achieving sustainability in the field of Information Technology. As most of the computing workloads are steadily migrating to cloud computing, the Cloud providers have started implementing Green Computing for their offerings, for their clients to choose from.

Understanding Green IT

Now let's look at Green IT and discuss the various stages in the equipment lifecycle at which care should be taken for.

Green Computing or Green IT aims to minimize the carbon footprint generated by Information Technology by efficiently designing, manufacturing, using, and disposing of IT resources. The objective is to have the least possible environmental impact. IT resources that need to be focused upon encompass a wide range of hardware, such as servers, monitors, printers, scanners, hard drives, routers, cables, and more.

Green Computing advocates for businesses to closely examine their IT department processes to assess the sustainability of their practices and strategies. By doing so, they can take substantial steps to reduce the negative impact of IT operations on the environment.

Over the past few decades, Green IT has been viewed as still a developing and evolving concept. Over the years, organizations have faced challenges in adopting Green IT due to factors such as insufficient awareness, higher initial investment requirements, prioritization of more immediate value-adding initiatives, and cultural resistance.

But more and more companies are now adopting Green IT for following reasons:

- Increased understanding of the impact on climate change. There is now sufficient metrics captured over the decades to understand the impact of the use of resources (like associated carbon footprint, emissions) on the environment. Organizations also understand the benefits from reduction in cost due to recycling and extended life of equipment.

- Regulatory compliance obligations and/or government incentives provided. This field is now more mature with regulatory and industry standards established to try control the impact. There are sometimes incentives offered for compliant organizations. For example, Green Grid's Cloud Operations Management (COmP) certification program, which provides a framework for improving cloud data center energy efficiency, and the Carbon Disclosure Project, which offers a platform for organizations to disclose and manage their greenhouse gas emissions. By leveraging these resources, organizations can effectively monitor and improve their sustainability performance and demonstrate their commitment to sustainability to stakeholders.
- Competitive Initiative. This shift towards sustainability is not only driven by environmental concerns but also by financial benefits, So, as more organizations have begun adopting these sustainability practices, it is becoming increasingly important for competitors to either adopt similar approaches or risk falling behind.
- Advancement in technology and increased technology know-how. This field is relatively mature now, as there have been many advancements in technology to support this. There are now tools and processes available for organizations to assess, evaluate, implement, monitor and control the sustainability impact of technology.
- Customer goodwill for sustainability. This refers to the positive sentiment and preference customers have for organizations that prioritize sustainability and demonstrate a commitment to reducing their environmental impact. Customers are increasingly concerned about the environmental impact of the products and services they use, and they are more likely to choose and remain loyal to companies that prioritize sustainability. Additionally, customers are often willing to pay a premium for sustainable products and services, providing a financial incentive for organizations to prioritize sustainability.

Green IT requires focus on all stages of the equipment's lifecycle.

Let's discuss this in detail below:

Manufacturing of equipment

Following are processes to be taken care of, during the manufacture of IT equipment, to reduce carbon footprint.

- Reduce the use of harmful materials for creating the equipment.
    - o Follow RoHS (Restriction of Hazardous Substances) directed limits

to restrict the amount and number of hazardous materials (lead, mercury, cadmium, etc.) used in manufacture of electronic and electrical equipment.

- o Reduce use of Brominated Flame Retardants (BFRs) and instead use alternatives like phosphorus-based flame retardants or non-halogenated flame retardants, which are less toxic.
- o Using recycled plastics and metals, as well as bio-based plastics made from renewable resources.
- o Instead of traditional PVC insulation, which can release harmful chemicals, opt for non-toxic alternatives such as cross-linked polyethylene (XLPE) or polyolefin.
- o Use of Low-Volatile Organic Compounds (VOC) or water-based coatings

- Increase recycling ability of digital devices.
  - o Comply with recycling regulations and standards, such as the EU's WEEE (Waste Electrical and Electronic Equipment).
  - o Choose materials that are easily recyclable, such as certain plastics, metals, and glass.
  - o Design for Disassembly where parts can be easily removed for repair or replacement.
  - o Use of standardized sub-components so that they have wider usage.
  - o Use automated sorting procedures to segregate disposable materials.
- Build energy efficient hardware.
  - o Use energy-efficient processes in the manufacturing phase to reduce the overall energy footprint of the hardware
  - o Use energy-efficient display technologies like LED and Implement adaptive brightness controls that adjust screen brightness based on ambient lighting conditions.
  - o Use operating systems and firmware that support and utilize advanced power management features.
  - o Use energy-efficient storage technologies such as solid-state drives (SSDs).
  - o Use advanced thermal materials to manage heat effectively and effectively dissipate heat to avoid unnecessary power consumption.
  - o Effective component design to minimize power leaks and use of processors with energy-saving features, such as dynamic frequency scaling.
- Ability to reuse or refurbish end-of-life equipment.

Usage of equipment

During the use, following aspects should be considered to take care for choosing the right equipment and use them effectively

- Use energy efficient and multi-functional devices, example:
  - Multi-Function-Printer which can do several activities like scanning, printing, copying.
  - Provide an option to use recycled paper when printing.
- Replace old equipment if not energy efficient - like using LCD instead of CRT monitors.
- Setup the data centers in locations that have favorable weather conditions resulting in consumption of less energy.
- Using AI, configure devices to auto-stop / turn off when not in use. This will avoid unnecessary running of components, for example, schedule auto turn-off development servers during non-work hours.
- Utilize resources when there is less load on them, which will result in sharing of computer, memory, networking, etc.
- Identify idle resources and take appropriate action to Reduce / Reuse / Recycle. Servers or components sitting idle will result in increased maintenance and operational costs. Regular audits need to be done to identify such resources.

Disposal of equipment

Once the equipment reaches its end-of-life, it should be disposed of responsibly. Care should be taken for effective data wiping prior to disposal.

- Identify devices that could be reused, refurbished, recycled, and those that need to be disposed of.
- Properly segregate items that should be disposed, based on their category. (e.g., batteries, plastics, metals) to facilitate recycling and recovery of valuable materials.
- Care should be taken to properly dispose electronic waste that contains harmful materials like mercury, lead, mercury, and cadmium to avoid environmental impact.
- Donate working resources. In case resources are being replaced with more powerful, more efficient ones or disposing of redundant resources - such equipment which are in working condition can be donated.
- Engage certified e-waste recyclers for processing, such as those compliant with R2 stands for Responsible Recycling.

Sustainable Cloud Computing

Now that we have understood the relevance of sustainability from a traditional IT setup, let's shift our focus to the Cloud perspective of the Green Computing. This presents a Point-Of-View of why cloud computing results in a relatively smaller carbon footprint and discuss the best practices to be followed

Studies from multiple cloud providers show what cloud datacenters have smaller Carbon Footprint than on-premises datacenters. This can be attributed to the following practices:

- **IT Operations Efficiency:** Cloud Datacenters can operate more efficiently because of leveraging large economies of scale in Cloud computing. They employ practices like dynamically provisioning resources and adopting virtualization to increase the efficiency of operations.
- **Better resource utilization:** Cloud datacenters have higher resource utilization as compared to individual on-premises datacenters. Cloud hosting is typically multitenancy which results in sharing of resources among multiple tenants with different demand patterns. There have been significant advances in system design patterns that has resulted in more efficient solutions. They also leverage latest server, hardware, and software technologies.
- **Datacenter equipment efficiency:** Advanced infrastructure technologies are used, and hardware components are tailored to specific needs of the services resulting in efficient energy utilization.
- **Potential for using Renewable electricity:** Due to largescale and continuous energy demands by the Cloud datacenters, there is potential for using renewable energy sources.

In addition to the above inherent features of Cloud that result in increased efficiencies, Green Cloud refers to the sustainable way of cloud computing that reduces energy demand and keeps control on the generation of e-waste in a way to address environmental issues.

The term "green cloud" signifies the practice of implementing and managing cloud computing services in a manner that minimizes environmental impact, conserves energy, and reduces carbon emissions. Green cloud computing strives to optimize resource utilization, enhance energy efficiency, and promote the adoption of renewable energy sources within cloud data centers. By embracing green cloud practices, organizations can significantly diminish their environmental footprint, cut operational expenses, and display their dedication to sustainability. Green cloud initiatives often entail implementing energy-efficient server designs, optimizing data center cooling systems, leveraging virtualization and containerization technologies, and employing cloud-based monitoring and automation tools to regulate energy consumption and minimize waste.

Best Practices for Green Cloud Computing

Similar to how Green IT is a collective responsibility at all phases of the equipment life cycle, Green Cloud Computing is a collective responsibility of all the parties involved in providing and consuming the services. Following are the categorizations based on the service provider / consumer.

Cloud provider responsibilities

Cloud service providers should take the following measures in order to increase the provisioning and operational efficiency of cloud services that are offered.

- Choose a data centre location that requires lesser energy consumption, like avoiding extreme hot desert locations. Example: Microsoft's Project Natick, was a research project to determine the feasibility of subsea datacenters powered by offshore renewable energy
- Promote the use of renewal energy in the datacenters.
- Use more efficient hardware and infrastructure. examples:
    - Using of dynamic voltage and frequency scaling
    - Using modern data storage devices (In comparison to the older HDD technology, new SSD devices use less power, can access data faster and even last longer until replacement).
    - Using optimized hardware, datacenters become more efficient and can minimize their energy demand.
- Workload shifting to avoid peak times – to shift noncritical workloads to quieter times to reduce network traffic. Or run during that time of the day when solar energy can be leveraged.

Service consumer responsibilities

Cloud Service Consumers have the responsibility to apply due diligence in choosing the appropriate services and follow best practices in designing the IT solutions.

- Opt for low carbon regions and those with less Green House Emissions (GHE)
- Reduce resource usage when not required (avoid running resources all day unless required)
- Sun and wind-based scheduling: Scheduled workloads at a time when there is use of renewable energy by the datacenters (where supported).
- Usage of Green criteria for choosing appropriate cloud solutions should be encouraged.
- Adopting Green computing architecture:
    - Use serverless services that support autoscaling.
    - Decouple computing and storage.
    - Build Microservices based solutions (which are independently scalable) as against monolith.

o Efficient data storage mechanisms like archiving unfrequently used data, using data compression techniques to reduce storage space. Define data retention policies and auto-clean data after a defined duration.

Monitoring Sustainability of cloud computing

Monitoring the sustainability of cloud computing entails regular tracking and evaluation of different components of cloud operations to guarantee they conform to environmental and efficiency objectives. This includes monitoring energy consumption, carbon emissions, resource utilization, and waste generation, among other metrics. By continuously monitoring and assessing these factors, organizations can identify areas for improvement, optimize resource usage, and make data-driven decisions to enhance sustainability and efficiency.

There are now ways available to measure a Cloud Providers' carbon footprint, and such information will help customers to understand the environmental impact of a given cloud architecture and the associated carbon footprint. This also helps in understanding the finer details like what amount of electricity will be used, the amount of CO2 emissions, etc. Based on such information, the Cloud Service Consumers can make an informed decision on the type and location of hosting their services on cloud and improve their solution design.

A critical aspect for the management is to understand how relevant and how important the low carbon footprint is, in the scope of a given solution. A starting and positive step in this direction would be to identify the sustainability relevance of an IT solution and assess the viability in accordance with the organization. This needs to be done in association with various Functional and Non-Functional criteria that are considered during the assessment and design phases of the project like performance, cost, efficiency, scalability, latency etc.

Most of the cloud providers provide ways to assess the carbon-footprint. Below are a few examples:

- **Microsoft Emissions Impact Dashboard**: https://www.microsoft.com/en-us/sustainability/emissions-impact-dashboard
- **Google Cloud Carbon Footprint**: https://cloud.google.com/carbon-footprint
- **AWS Customer Carbon Footprint Tool**: https://aws.amazon.com/aws-cost-management/aws-customer-carbon-footprint-tool/
- **IBM Cloud's carbon calculator**: https://cloud.ibm.com/docs/billing-usage?topic=billing-usage-what-is-cloud-calc

There are also tools available to assist in a Hybrid Cloud scenario, that help to assess and compare the overall emissions of the entire portfolio. They can typically show information in a dashboard, for example, by dividing resources into various types – compute-clusters / DB etc. Below are a few examples of such tools

- **Cloud Carbon Footprint**: Opensource Cloud Carbon Emissions Measurement and Analysis Tool https://www.cloudcarbonfootprint.org/
- **Texture for Green Cloud Assessment**: https://txture.io/en/product/green-cloud-assessment

Conclusion

Green computing has not yet fully addressed the rapid growth of IT equipment in our digital ecosystem. More efforts are required to popularize Green IT alternatives to ensure environmental sustainability. To maximize influence, there should be enhanced awareness and affordability of energy-efficient options.

For customers relying on Cloud computing services, historically, the emphasis has been mainly on Non-Functional attributes such as performance, cost, efficiency, scalability, and latency. However, it is crucial to also consider the green criteria. And, from the perspective of the Cloud service providers, there is a need for amplified concentration on offering Green Solutions accessible for utilization.

References

- https://txture.io/en/blog/green-cloud
- https://www.techtarget.com/searchcio/definition/green-IT-green-information-technology
- https://www.ibm.com/blog/green-computing/
- https://download.microsoft.com/download/7/3/9/739bc4ad-a855-436e-961d-9c95eb51daf9/microsoft_cloud_carbon_study_2018.pdf
- https://d39w7f4ix9f5s9.cloudfront.net/d1/80/283b833847df8ee4fe9661e0dd8f/11061-aws-451research-advisory-bw-cloudefficiency-eu-2021-r2-final-2.pdf

JOIN US ON THE
ARCCHIE PUBLICATIONS
DISCORD SERVER

Connect with fellow readers, authors, and enthusiasts to discuss all things related to our publications and the exciting world of AI, programming, and learning. Share your insights, ask questions, and engage in vibrant discussions to expand your knowledge and inspire creativity. Take advantage of this opportunity to be part of a dynamic community dedicated to exploring the frontiers of technology and innovation. Join our Discord Server today and be part of the ARCCHIE Publications community!

https://discord.gg/z26SenmpEt